HUBBLE REVEALS CREATION

HUBBLE REVEALS CREATION
By An Awe-Inspiring Power

J. PAUL HUTCHINS

Imagination
Publishing

IMAGINATION PUBLISHING
Orlando, Florida

This publication is designed to provide general, as well as detailed, information about the subject matter. It is sold with the understanding that the publisher and author are not scientists. Any information pertaining to the subject matter was gathered through research from various scientific documents published by NASA and associated organizations, websites, and astronomy publications. The information presented by the author is deemed to be accurate but not guaranteed to be so in all instances.

This book is intended to highlight the Awe-Inspiring space images and scientific data that are daily pouring in from space telescopes orbiting high above the Earth, as a testament to the Superior Imagination that surely went into the design of all these heavenly bodies. Any references or comments to the Scriptural quotes contained herein is for the purpose of drawing a parallel between man's exploration of space and Scriptural passages written thousands of years ago, and are the expressed views of the author only.

Hutchins, J. Paul, 1954-
    Hubble reveals creation : by an awe-inspiring power / J. Paul Hutchins. —
Orlando, Fla. : Imagination Publishing, c2012.

        p. ; cm.
        ISBN: 978-09817123-5-2
        Includes index.

        1. Creation. 2. Cosmology. 3. Intelligent design (Teleology) 4. Hubble
Space Telescope (Spacecraft) 5. Astronomy—Religious aspects—Christianity.
6. God (Christianity)—Proof, Cosmological. I. Title.

BL253 .H884 2011   2011930172
231.7/652—dc22   1107

Printed in China

For more information go to:
http://www.HubbleRevealsCreation.com

CONTENTS

ACT V: A GRAND ARCHITECT
REVEALED AND COMPLETED
A Special Star is Born

POWER BEYOND COMPREHENSION

CREATIVE IMAGINATION

THE GALLERY OF A FORMERLY UNKNOWN ARTIST WITH SUPREME IMAGINATION

For more information go to:

http://www.HubbleRevealsCreation.com

INTRODUCTION

IN WHAT IS SURE TO INSPIRE YOUR IMAGINATION, *Hubble Reveals Creation* meticulously details how the world-famous Hubble telescope is now revealing that the Universe was created through Intelligent Design by an Incomprehensible Power with Supreme Imagination. While it quotes from the book of Genesis and Isaiah, *Hubble Reveals Creation* is not about religion; rather it is a commonsense look at what Man's Insatiable Quest to the Stars is revealing about an Awe-Inspiring act of Creation.

It reveals how the Hubble and Spitzer telescopes have captured a scientific footprint of planet formation that appears to confirm the Genesis account of creation to be scientifically accurate.

It uncovers a Divine Invitation extended to man twenty-seven hundred years ago to investigate the stars. This invitation challenged mankind to find anyone equal in power to the One who created all the stars.

It reveals how man, with the invention of the telescope in 1609 embarked upon an insatiable quest to the stars as if he were being drawn to them by an invisible magnetic force, and is now spending tens of billions of dollars and hundreds of millions of man-hours each year in response to this intriguing invitation.

It details how this quest culminated with the invention of the Hubble Space Telescope that is now filming the Greatest Drama in Human History, the Creation of an Awe-Inspiring Universe, as it reveals an Incomprehensible Power without equal!

In cinematic fashion and simple layman terms, J. Paul Hutchins presents a real-life drama, telling an awe-inspiring story of how the universe was formed. You will be inspired by more than 145 full-color images of beautiful nebula, stars, and majestic galaxies. You will get a glimpse into the incomprehensible power behind the universe.

The author's intent is to inspire people who possess a logical reasoning mind that recognize nothing comes into existence devoid of imagination, to reaffirm their convictions, leaving little room for doubt that the Universe was brought to us through Intelligent Design and Supreme Imagination by a power incomprehensible to the human mind! The intriguing and compelling story He presents may just change the way you look at our universe, and man's future role in it.

A DIVINE INVITATION

"To whom will you compare me? Who is my equal?" asks the Holy One.
Look up into the heavens. Who created all the stars? He brings them out like
an army, one after another, calling each by its name. Because of his great
power and incomparable strength, not a single one is missing.
                                                               —Isaiah 40:25, 26

WHEN THE ANCIENT PROPHET Isaiah transcribed the words to this Divine Invitation, he could not have imagined the elevated meaning those words would acquire as a result of man's expanded imagination later on in history.

On the following pages is a real-life drama being played out like a silent motion picture—one frame at a time. Each frame tells its own awe-inspiring story. Collectively, they reveal the Grandest Story ever told: the Creation of the Universe in detail never before revealed.

What I present to you in this book is merely what I perceive, through my own imagination, as to how this Grand Drama came into view through man's use of imagination. It began with the invention of the telescope that turned into an insatiable quest to the stars. Also, I am demonstrating how imagination plays an intriguing role in the creation of all things, including our incredible universe. You and I find ourselves at the center of this story, as if we had a front row seat in front of a super-IMAX screen, taking in all the drama being presented.

As we each enter the theater and take our seats, we have a choice to make. Either we recognize that the unfolding drama is being brought to us by a Superior Architect with Supreme Imagination, power, and dynamic energy far beyond our comprehension or we decide it came about randomly on its

own, devoid of intelligent design and imagination. Regardless of your choice, the invitation to behold wonderful things no human eyes have ever seen has been graciously extended to each of us.

It is my desire that as you embark on this journey to the stars, you will take the time to meditate on the implications of the simple yet profound words Isaiah penned so long ago.

To understand how this drama came to be and is now being played out, we first need to look at this curious faculty we call imagination and what role it has played to bring this drama into view for the entire world to see. We must come to understand how the use of Supreme Imagination can be the only logical explanation for the Grandest Drama ever beheld by human eyes.

I invite you to sit back and enjoy an awe-inspiring view as you explore the incredible universe, expand your imagination, and ponder the limitless possibilities for our future as you respond to that ancient invitation to *"Look up into the heavens,"* and see *"Who created all the stars?"*

Who conceived this curious thing
we call Imagination?

ACT I

IMAGINATION

THE DRIVING FORCE BEHIND ALL CREATIVE WORKS

> "Imagination is everything. It is the preview of life's coming attractions." Albert Einstein (1879-1955)

All things created, from the smallest to the largest, are first conceived in the mind and then driven by the force of imagination to make them real. Everything achieved by man and considered great by many was driven by imagination—the dynamic force that shapes our world.

Imagination is the force that drove the artist to first create in his mind and then bring to reality works of art like the *Mona Lisa* (Leonardo da Vinci) and *Water Lilies* (Claude Monet).

It is the driving force that impelled the architect to first create in his mind and then bring to reality great works like the Great Pyramid of Cheops (Egyptian Pharaoh Khufu of the Fourth Dynasty) and the Eiffel Tower (Alexandre Gustave Eiffel).

It is the force that drove the inventor to first conceive in his mind and then bring to reality the dream of human flight (brothers Orville and Wilbur Wright) and the phonograph (Thomas Edison).

It is the force that drove the musician to first compose in his mind and then bring to life—*The Brandenburg Concertos* (Johann Sebastian Bach) and *Pastoral* (Ludwig van Beethoven).

It is the force that drove the scientist to discover the law of gravity—(Isaac Newton) and the Law of Relativity (Albert Einstein).

It is the force that drove the writer/poet to first create in his mind and then bring to life—*Romeo and Juliet* and *Hamlet* (William Shakespeare) and "I'm Nobody! Who are you?" (Emily Dickinson).

These works, along with all others, were inspired by creative imagination and, in one way or another, have shaped our world. The entire life experience of man has revealed that nothing we have designed, invented, conceived, or brought into existence, came about void of imagination. This fact brings us to this very important question: If man's imagination is the driving force that shapes our world, then whose imagination is the driving force that shaped the universe?

> *"The true sign of intelligence is not knowledge but imagination."*
> Albert Einstein

ACT II

IMAGINATION

THE DRIVING FORCE THAT SHAPES OUR WORLD

Imagination
The Driving Force That Shapes Our World

A WORLD WITHOUT IMAGINATION would be no world at all, sad to say. In fact, our world would be a dull and boring place if it were not for this intriguing gift we all possess.

Imagination shapes our world. From the artist to the inventor, each is driven by a small inner voice that inspires him or her to do the impossible, the unheard of. They are driven to reach beyond their limits to discover and devise all things new. Imagination has given us variety, excitement, and the anticipation of what may materialize in the future.

From the earliest days of our existence, humans have taken raw materials from the Earth and, through imagination, formed and shaped them from basic materials into useful devices, just as a potter or sculptor takes a lump of clay and, through his or her imagination, creates something beautiful and useful.

In the beginning, man ground stones and shaped them into tools. In time, he learned how to melt copper and steel ore and to forge them into axes for cutting trees and tools to cultivate the ground. These advances provided shelter, simple houses, and food.

With each passing generation, more raw materials were taken from the Earth and turned into many useful devices. Through the imagination of following generations, those devices were improved upon and eventually replaced. With each generation, the human imagination grew stronger and became more creative.

Every year, we see thousands of new products and ideas brought into the marketplace by highly imaginative men and women. It is more and more difficult to keep up with all the new things coming at us. The same can be said about the arts, architecture, science, astronomy, literature, film, and every other field of endeavor known to man. It seems that man has been blessed with an unlimited imagination.

If you were to compare human knowledge and imagination today to that of those who lived four thousand years ago, you would find that there is no comparison. The human mind has had the benefit of a much greater reservoir of knowledge and experience to draw upon, gathered over the millennia. Knowledge is the fuel that feeds the human imagination and inspires it to create new things. It is clear that when a thinking person imagines big, what they imagined often takes on a life of its own. One good example of this was the life of the Italian physicist Galileo, who lived from 1564 to 1642. Through his imagination and experimentation he improved upon the telescope. Drawing upon the knowledge of others in the same field of interest, he pointed his new telescope to the heavens and began to study the night sky in a way that no one before him ever had.

In his observations, he discovered the four largest moons of Jupiter. Also, through his studies and observations, he began to realize, like Nicolaus Copernicus and Johannes Kepler, that the Earth moved around the Sun; not the other way around, as commonly thought. He recognized that there was a much greater body of stars than previously believed. His curiosity led to a new way of looking at the world and the heavens above. Nevertheless, his imagination and abilities were limited due to the paucity of scientific knowledge and tools available at the time. However, he lit the fuse and sparked a race to the stars that resulted four centuries later in the discovery of a Universe even more Awe-Inspiring than previously celebrated.

Expanded Imagination

In the generations after Galileo, many improvements were made to the telescope; and in the 1920s, man's imagination began to kick into high gear. Still, most scientists considered a space telescope pure science fiction. However, some were seriously exploring the idea. Rocket pioneer Hermann Oberth, for example, speculated about orbiting telescopes in his writings, and scientist Robert Goddard began testing his newly invented liquid-fuel rockets.

As these men were pushing the technological envelope, Edwin Hubble was unveiling new heavenly horizons. Before Hubble came along, astronomers had a restricted view of the universe, believing that the only galaxy in the heavens was our Milky Way. But Hubble used the latest technology, a powerful one-hundred-inch telescope, and made some startling discoveries that changed our concept of the cosmos.

First, he observed that galaxies existed beyond the Milky Way. Then he found that those galaxies were flying away from each other, an observation that helped him determine that the universe was expanding.

It takes powerful telescopes to study the uncharted territories of the vast cosmos. But it became increasingly clear to astronomers that the Earth's atmosphere distorted starlight, which made it difficult to obtain razor-sharp views of celestial objects.

The idea of placing a telescope in space, above Earth's turbulent air, had been imagined and kicked around for several years. Scientists pondered how to transport a telescope into space. The rocket technology pioneered by Oberth and

Goddard and revolutionized by the Germans during World War II became the means of transportation.

After scientists figured out the means, they focused on coming up with the money to develop and build a space telescope. The newly established National Aeronautics and Space Administration (NASA), created in 1958, and well-known American astronomers such as Lyman Spitzer, began championing the cause, trying to convince the United States Congress that such a project was useful. In 1977, Congress finally agreed to allocate the money; but it took a decade of research, planning, and testing before NASA successfully launched its first space observatory. Two decades passed before NASA launched the Hubble space telescope on April 24, 1990. This initiative has expanded our heavenly vistas far more than its namesake ever dreamed.

Like a young child trying to climb out of its crib, man is determined, now more than ever, to see what is on the outside. His curiosity and imagination are driving him to do what seemed to former generations as impossible. In his mind the railing is not too high; he will figure it out!

Imagination is proving to be man's way out, and a doorway to a world beyond imagination. The first discovery of that doorway was made when the telescope was invented and improved upon, through the use of imagination early in our history. Since Galileo, man has continued to improve upon the telescope and taken additional steps toward understanding the heavens above, as if they were calling to him. With Hubble, Spitzer, and other modern-day telescopes, it is as if we are ascending a stairway right up into the heavens for a front-row view of a Grand Drama of Creation in progress. There is no doubt that imagination will continue to play a key role in the development of new ways to explore the awe-inspiring Heavenly night sky, and take further thrilling steps that will bring us closer to understanding our incredible universe.

As one looks at the photos and the body of evidence gathered since Hubble's launch, it becomes clear that we have ascended ever closer to a world that is beyond human imagination. It is as if one were climbing a long winding staircase, twisting and turning past galaxies and stars too numerous to count. There are natural phenomena too bizarre for us to fully understand as we make our way back to the beginning of the universe. Like a wide-eyed child, we can hardly wait to see what is around the corner to excite and enlighten us!

When we review how telescope technology has progressed, we find that the road, at times, has been bumpy but man's burning desire to learn ever more of our universe has never dampened in the slightest way. With every obstacle he encountered along the way man tapped deeper into his imagination to develop a solution which always inspired new technology that has taken him closer to the ultimate discovery of our incredible universe and an Awe-Inspiring Power.

ACT III

MAN'S INSATIABLE QUEST TO THE STARS

Eyes To See

Eyes to See an Awe-Inspiring Power

FOR MILLENNIA, MAN HAS GAZED at the night sky with his naked eyes. He has dreamed of what must lie beyond the darkness amongst the glimmering stars, as he long harbored a burning desire to understand their source. Looking back on the history of the telescope, each of us must recognize we have been given a gift of sight beyond anything Galileo could have imagined. This is all a direct result of man's imagination. We now see images of the universe through sophisticated telescopes that are so jaw-dropping awe-inspiring they are just short of inspired visions. What Isaiah must have seen and written about two millennia earlier was no doubt an inspired vision of the reality we now behold through the eye of the Hubble telescope.

The telescope had a very humble beginning. It evolved from the spyglass used by sailors to spy on distant ships. This, in turn, had evolved from the invention of eyeglasses. Hans Lippershey, in the Netherlands, is generally credited with the earliest recorded design for an optical telescope (a refracting telescope) in 1608, although it is unclear if he actually invented it. A master lens grinder, his work with optical devices grew out of his work as a spectacle maker. One story contends that Lippershey got the idea for his spyglass invention from children playing in his shop. They held two eyeglass lenses up together and discovered they could see the weathervane atop a distant church.

This small, simple invention, accidentally set man's imagination ablaze and took him to a world beyond imagination, a world unknown to previous generations. When Galileo improved upon Lippershey's invention and turned his newly improved telescope toward the night sky, it was if some invisible force was compelling it skyward—much like a compass needle is compelled to point to the magnetic north. With each passing generation, the size and magnification of the telescope grew, as did the compulsion to point them skyward in search of what was hidden beyond the night sky. While some were driven by their thirst for fame or prestige, others were propelled by a sheer quest to know what existed out there in this bold, new world.

> *By taking our sense of sight far beyond the realm of our forebears' imagination, these wonderful instruments, the telescopes, open the way to a deeper and more perfect understanding of nature.* —René Descartes, 1637

Galileo devoted his time to improving and perfecting the telescope and soon succeeded in producing telescopes of greatly increased power. His telescope was a simple instrument compared to the colossal telescopes of today. It was a small tube with two lenses—the primary convex lens that curved outward, and the concave eyepiece lens that curved inward. Nevertheless, it set the principle for telescopes to come. It would be through the use of lenses and later mirrors to gather more light than the human eye could collect on its own, focus it, and form an image through magnification that would make it possible to seeing distant objects as if they were close up. The word *telescope* was coined in 1611 by the Greek mathematician Giovanni Demisiani for one of Galileo Galilei's far-seeing instruments.

Galileo quickly realized through his observations with this intriguing new instrument that the world he observed was the very sun-centered world that Nicolaus Copernicus had theorized about in his book *De Revolutionibus Orbium Coelestium*. Copernicus had printed it in 1543 in his revolutionary rejection of the popular belief that the Earth was at the center of the universe.

For the first time in history it was as if a veil had been lifted for all eyes to see what Isaiah had seen and written about some twenty-three hundred years earlier. Now, more than ever before, man's desire to know was being fueled by the things this new technology was revealing. It was if a fuse had been lit, never to be extinguished.

If you look at the insatiable development of the telescope from Galileo onward, each generation studied the men and telescopes that preceded them. They used their own imaginations and thirst for knowledge or fame to improve upon the existing technology. They continued to devise a better way to view the night sky in a way that had never been revealed. From a simple, small, 1.5-centimeter-wide aperture device weighing only a few pounds, the telescope evolved over a four-hundred-year period to colossal telescopes of today weighing hundreds of tons with reflectors measuring over ten meters in diameter. Today there are computer-driven, laser- and GPS-guided, ground-based telescopes costing hundreds of millions of dollars to flying space telescopes costing billions of dollars with thirty- and forty-meter ground-based telescopes on the drawing board for the near future.

The history and list of telescopes on the following pages in no way represents all the telescopes and developments that have taken place over the past few centuries that have led us to this point in our quest. The purpose of this historical account is not to bore you with history but to unequivocally show that the development of this particular instrument, out of all of man's inventions, appears as though it were part of some master plan to reveal to all humanity a Grand Creation by an Awe-Inspiring and Powerful Creator. It will also highlight man's obsession with the telescope, which has grown to a fever pitch in just the last few decades as this quest has intensified with the introduction of microprocessors and other sophisticated equipment.

There are so many telescopes in use around the world today with capabilities too numerous to count. There are also numerous satellites, space probes, and space agencies dedicated to this quest. Billions of dollars are spent each year, along with millions of man-hours dedicated to searching the night sky.

The two telescopes that have had the most profound impact on humanity, as of this writing, would be Galileo's telescope that started us on this quest and the Hubble space telescope that has revealed a Grand Drama of Creation by an Incomprehensible Power. No one can deny the evidence presented by this history of the telescope. Man's drive to learn more about the stars has now become an obsession for individuals, governments, and space agencies all around the globe. They have joined the race as if some invisible force was drawing each passing generation deeper and deeper into this insatiable quest with an intense burning desire to see further and further as man's awe and knowledge of this incredible universe deepens.

Each day and night the heavens are bubbling forth in unspoken words with endless amounts of information that have been hidden from man for millennia that is just now coming to light through the eye of the Hubble telescope. Hubble transmits about 120 gigabytes of science data back to Earth every week. That is equal to about 3,600 feet (1,097 meters) of books on a shelf. The data gathered thus far by Hubble will take many decades to glean and unravel.

Like buried treasures, the outposts of the universe have beckoned to the adventurous from immemorial times. Princes and potentates, political or industrial, equally with men of science, have felt the lure of the unchartered seas of space, and through their provision of instrumental means the sphere of exploration has rapidly widened. —George Ellery Hale

As you review this history of the telescope, four things become abundantly clear: (1) There is no limit to man's imagination in devising new technology to reach his goals. (2) Man's original curiosity with the stars has turned into an insatiable quest in which no investment of time or money is too large. (3) Some unexplainable force seems to be driving man in this quest with it intensifying with each new generation. (4) Man's insatiable quest to the stars will never be quenched because we have come upon an incomprehensible and endless universe where each new astronomical discovery draws us in deeper, confounding former theories and raising more unanswered questions. These, in turn, fuel man's imagination to develop new ways to probe ever deeper for the answers to the new questions.

Man's Quest to the Stars

MAN'S EARLY FASCINATION

From **early** times, **man** has had a fascination with the stars in the night sky. The seasons became important as different stellar patterns would appear in the sky during different times of the year. In the spring, Virgo and her accompanying constellations would signal the time to prepare the earth, to plant crops, and to be wary of floods.

In the fall, Orion rises to indicate time to harvest and to prepare for winter. Early astronomers used many kinds of instruments and structures to study the heavens. All were basically tools for measuring or calculating the positions of objects in the sky, including the Sun.

EARLY WRITINGS ABOUT THE STARS

The **early Biblical writers** made mention of the stars or referenced the heavens hundreds of times, indicating their keen interest in the stars in the night sky. They expressed certainty as to who was responsible for them. Those writers, including Isaiah, attributed the creation of all the stars to their God whose name according to the oldest Hebrew manuscripts was written with four Hebrew consonants called the Tetragrammaton (יהוה).

MAN'S INTEREST BECOMES A SCIENCE

With the passing centuries, man's fascination with the stars continued in conjunction with the study of philosophy, mathematics, and natural science. These later coalesced into astronomy, with men like Socrates, Plato, Aristotle, Aristarchus, Ptolemy, and **Copernicus** who developed a heliocentric model of the solar system which retained the notion of perfect circular motion, but placed the Sun at the center and established the proper order of the planets outward from the Sun that challenged the religious beliefs of his day.

(1609) A TURNING POINT WITH A MAGNETIC DRAW

The year 1609 marked a turning point in man's fascination with the stars. **Galileo** made improvements to a new invention called the *spyglass* by increasing it from an eight-power- to a twenty-power magnification. Galileo then used his imagination and fascination of the stars to turn his telescope skyward.

That single act opened up a whole new world that would spark an insatiable quest to the stars. A race soon developed to build bigger and better telescopes in order to understand this newfound world as if it were somehow calling to us to have a closer look. The race took two directions early on, one with the Galileo-style **refractor** telescope and the other with the Newton-style reflector telescope.

(1668) NEWTON MAKES A BREAKTHROUGH

When the Galileo-style refractor telescopes grew excessively long and increasingly difficult to handle, telescopes were ready for a new design. This design came courtesy of **Sir Isaac Newton**. He investigated the refraction of light, demonstrating that a prism could decompose white light into a spectrum of colors, and that a lens and a second prism could recompose the multicolored spectrum into white light.

The images produced by this new type of telescope were free from chromatic aberration (i.e., the rings of color that surrounded bright objects). He changed the primary lens to a mirror and launched a new class of telescopes called **reflectors**, which used a reflecting mirror.

(1673) TELESCOPES GROW TO 150 FEET IN LENGTH

With the acceptance of the astronomical telescope, a "telescope race" quickly developed. Beginning in the 1640s, the length of telescopes began to increase. From the typical Galilean telescope of five or six feet in length, astronomical telescopes rose to lengths of fifteen or twenty feet by the middle of the century.

By 1647, **Johannes Hevelius**, a Polish brewer and councilor, had built a twelve-foot-long telescope in an attempt to improve his view of the sky. That was just the beginning. In 1670, Hevelius's knowledge of the way **refracting** telescopes worked pushed him to create longer and longer telescopes that eventually stretched to 150 feet.

(1686) A TELESCOPE WITHOUT A TUBE

In 1686, Christopher Huygens, a Dutch astronomer, decided to stop using long tubes altogether because of the inherent problem with long-tube telescopes. He mounted his primary lens in a short iron tube and attached it to a high pole. He mounted the eyepiece in another small tube on the ground, and ran a length of cord between the two to help line them up. This left him with a 123-foot open-air telescope. Huygens' telescope didn't work well because it was difficult to line up the lenses on a dark night. His invention did not catch on very well with other astronomers.

(1721) SMALLER, MORE ACCURATE, AND MORE POWERFUL TELESCOPES

John Hadley, born in London, began to experiment with the grinding and polishing of metal. He managed to polish his metal mirror so that it had an approximate parabolic shape, avoiding the distortion in previous telescopes with spherical curves.

By 1721, he was successful in making a six-inch diameter Newtonian **reflector** telescope with a focal length of sixty-two inches. Hadley's shorter telescope could be completely enclosed in a metal tube and easily moved to view the sky. Because refractor telescopes were so long, they were difficult to adjust and maneuver.

Equally important as the telescope's parabolic mirror was its mounting. Telescopes have to track objects across the sky as the Earth turns. Hadley developed what is now called an altitude-azimuth mount which made it easier for the astronomer to keep the object in view.

(1789) REFLECTING TELESCOPES REACH FORTY-EIGHT INCHES IN DIAMETER

Sir William Herschel was a German musician, born in Hanover, England, who became obsessed with astronomy. The telescope race really began to heat up by the late 1770s, when Herschel had built several reflectors. His most successful one had a six-and-a-quater-inch mirror that was seven feet long. He used this telescope to compile the first substantial catalog of binary stars and, in 1781, he discovered the planet Uranus.

Since astronomers' design goals had changed with improvements in the **reflecting** telescope, the point was to build larger mirrors. The mirror size determined how powerful the telescope would be, so Herschel's goal was to make them bigger and better. In the fall of 1789 he began using a forty-foot telescope with a forty-eight-inch mirror and found two additional satellites of Saturn.

(1824) A TELESCOPE THAT TRACKED STARS AUTOMATICALLY

Joseph von Fraunhofer was the most talented lens crafter of his time. He constructed a nine-and-a-half-inch lens for the Russian Dorpat Observatory. Using this lens, Russian astronomers were able to discern over 2,000 new double stars. The fourteen-foot long "Great Dorpat **Refractor**" was noted not only for the high quality of its lenses but also for its mounting. It was the first example of what became known as *equatorial mounting*, which allowed the telescope to be rotated toward any part of the sky.

The great advantage of Fraunhofer's equatorial mounting was that the polar axis was continuously rotated by a clock mechanism, allowing it to track stars automatically. This improvement proved essential when photography was introduced into astronomy in the latter part of the nineteenth century.

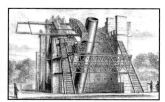

(1845) THE LEVIATHAN OF PARSONSTOWN

Irish nobleman **William Parsons**, the third Earl of Rosse, wanted to build the world's largest telescope. When he built a seventy-two-inch metal mirror weighing four tons and a tube fifty-four-feet long, the public was so impressed by the **reflector** they called it the Leviathan of Parsonstown. Lord Rosse's telescope remained the world's largest for the rest of the century until the construction of the 100-inch Hooker Telescope in 1917.

Using this telescope he saw and cataloged a large number of galaxies and was the first to see the spiral structure of what was later known as the Whirlpool Galaxy. Parsons improved the techniques of casting, grinding, and polishing large telescope mirrors from speculum metal, and constructed steam-powered grinding machines for parabolic mirrors.

(1847) LARGE TELESCOPES MAKE THEIR WAY TO THE UNITED STATES

Although interest in astronomy at **Harvard** dated to the seventeenth century, it was not until 1843, when a comet of surpassing size and splendor appeared, that public interest in astronomy was enormous enough to raise funds for a truly first-class observatory. In 1847, a fifteen-inch-diameter lens for the **Great Refractor** was ordered from Merz and Mahler of Munich and dedicated at the Harvard College Observatory.

This was the world's largest **refractor** for the next twenty years. Observatory director William Cranch Bond, a watchmaker, used clockwork to keep the telescope steadily focused on the Moon as it crossed the sky. He cast the Moon's image on a photographic plate, and took the first picture of the Moon taken by a telescope.

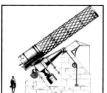

(1868) THE WISDOM OF GLASS MIRRORS OVER METAL

The **Great Melbourne Telescope** was constructed by Howard Grubb in Dublin in 1868 for the Melbourne Observatory. The telescope was designed to explore the nebulae visible from the southern hemisphere. Its primary task was to document whether any changes had occurred in the nebulae since they had been charted by John Herschel in the 1830s. It was a **reflecting** telescope with a forty-eight-inch Cassegrain metal mirror.

By 1877, the metal mirrors were so tarnished that they needed to be polished; they never worked well thereafter. For many years, astronomers avoided making large reflecting telescopes; this marked a turning point in telescope building. This would be the last large reflecting telescope built with a metal mirror.

(1873) U.S. FEDERAL GOVERNMENT JOINS THE QUEST

The U.S. Naval Observatory's twenty-six-inch "Great Equatorial" **refracting** telescope was completed in 1873 at a cost of $50,000. It was the largest working refracting telescope in the world for a decade and took the telescope race to another level—with government involvement.

The lens and mounting were made by the renowned firm of Alvan Clark & Sons of Cambridgeport, Massachusetts, and the great telescope was erected on the grounds of the old Naval Observatory site in the Foggy Bottom section of Washington. It was from this site, in August of 1877, that astronomer Asaph Hall discovered the two moons of Mars, Phobos and Deimos, with the "Great Equatorial Telescope."

(1888) THE GREAT LICK THIRTY-SIX-INCH REFRACTOR TELESCOPE

James Lick, an heirless San Francisco businessman, decided to immortalize himself by funding the world's biggest telescope. His wish was granted after his death when Alvan Clark & Sons were given the contract to produce a thirty-six-inch lens for the giant telescope on Mount Hamilton near Santa Cruz, California.

The Lick Observatory was the world's first permanently occupied mountain-top observatory. The thirty-six-inch refracting telescope on Mt. Hamilton was Earth's largest **refracting** telescope during the period from when it saw first light on January 3, 1888, until the construction of Yerkes in 1897.

The excellent quality of the thirty-six-inch telescope, combined with Mount Hamilton's excellent observing conditions, helped Lick Observatory become one of the world's premier astronomy institutions. Lick had also helped start a trend of building major American telescopes under the relatively cloudless western skies.

(1895) YERKES FORTY-INCH REFRACTOR

George Ellery Hale, an American astronomer, may have been the greatest American science entrepreneur of his time. He inspired, organized, and helped find funding for three of the most important observatories in the history of astronomy. Hale convinced the Chicago tycoon Charles Tyson Yerkes to finance the largest achromatic **refractor** that would ever be created: the Yerkes telescope.

The telescope, with its moving parts and counterweights, weighed over twenty tons, yet it was so well-balanced that small motors could easily move it to point at any part of the sky. The Yerkes would be the last of the great **refractors**. The lenses had grown as large as they could; for future advances, astronomers would return to reflector telescopes.

(1908) THE REBIRTH OF LARGE REFLECTING TELESCOPES

Astronomer George Ellery Hale chose American optician and telescope maker George W. Ritchey to design the sixty-inch reflecting telescope at Mount Wilson Observatory. At the time, it could boast of being the largest operational telescope in the world. The **sixty-inch reflector** became one of the most productive and successful telescopes in astronomical history.

Ritchey introduced the Coudé system, a novel way of deflecting the light outside the telescope to instruments too heavy to be attached to the tube. This enabled photography and spectroscopy, using cameras and spectroscopes. Its design and light-gathering power allowed the pioneering of spectroscopic analysis, parallax measurements, nebula photography, and photometric photography. The giant reflecting telescope soon supplanted the refracting telescope as the astronomer's workhorse.

(1917) MAN'S VIEW OF THE UNIVERSE CHANGES AT 100 INCHES

The sixty-inch telescope at California's Mount Wilson Observatory was not big enough to suit astronomer George Ellery Hale. Hale wanted a telescope that could collect more light. So, even as the sixty-inch reflecting telescope was being built, Hale was looking for the funding for a **reflector** with a **100-inch mirror**.

The "Hooker 100" telescope saw first light in 1917 and was equipped in 1919 with a special attachment, an optical astronomical interferometer developed by Albert Michelson. The mechanism incorporated a mercury float to provide smooth operation. All motions of the telescope, including its dome and shutters, were electrically controlled by thirty motors.

Edwin Hubble performed his critical calculations from work on the 100-inch telescope. He determined that some nebulae were actually galaxies outside our Milky Way Galaxy. Hubble, assisted by Milton L. Humason, discovered the presence of the redshift that indicated the universe is expanding—now recognized as one of the great scientific discoveries. Many observations since have confirmed the model of an expanding universe that Hubble validated.

(1932) A NEW WAY TO LOOK AT THE UNIVERSE

In 1931, Karl Guthe Jansky (considered one of the founding figures of radio astronomy), an engineer with Bell Telephone Laboratories, was assigned the job of identifying sources of static that might interfere with **radio telephone** service. Jansky discovered an unexplained "faint hiss" that originated well beyond the Earth's atmosphere. A fascinating find, it repeated on a cycle of twenty-three hours and fifty-six minutes.

By comparing his observations with optical astronomical maps, Jansky concluded that the radiation was coming from the Milky Way Galaxy. When Grote Reber, an amateur astronomer, learned of Karl Jansky's work, he decided this was the field he wanted to work in. In the summer of 1937, Reber decided to build his own radio telescope in his backyard in Wheaton.

Reber's radio telescope was considerably more advanced than Jansky's but it was not until his third attempt in 1938 that he detected signals from outer space at 160 MHz that confirmed Jansky's discovery. The radio telescope race had begun!

(1949) HALE 200-INCH REFLECTOR TELESCOPE

In 1928, Hale began raising money once again, this time for a **reflecting telescope** with a 200-inch Cassegrain mirror. The primary mirror for the Hale telescope was cast in 1934 at Corning Glass Works, using a new material called Pyrex. This had been chosen for its low expansion qualities so the large mirror would not distort the images produced when it changed shape due to temperature variations. This was a problem that had plagued earlier large telescopes. The mirror was coated with aluminum—a material that, unlike silver, does not tarnish.

Hale would never see the finished reflector. He died in 1938. In recognition of his tireless work, leadership, and dedicated vision this powerful telescope was named in honor of him. The construction and delivery of the Pyrex glass disk for the Palomar 200-inch reflector in 1936 marked a watershed in the history of astronomy.

The dome, 200-inch telescope, and its moving parts weighed over 1,500 tons. It was the world's largest effective telescope for forty-five years. As powerful as this telescope was, its view was distorted by Earth's atmosphere which set into motion once again, man's imagination to overcome a seemly insurmountable obstacle, paving the way for a space telescope.

(1964) COSMIC MICROWAVE BACKGROUND DISCOVERED

Robert Woodrow Wilson an American astronomer, 1978 Nobel laureate in physics, who along with Arno Allan Penzias, an American physicist, discovered in 1964 the cosmic microwave background radiation (CMB).

While working on a new type of antenna at Bell Labs they found a source of noise in the atmosphere that they could not explain. After removing all potential sources of noise, including pigeon droppings on the antenna, the noise was finally identified as CMB, which served as important corroboration of the Big Bang theory.

Cosmic background radiation is well explained as radiation left over from an early stage in the development of the universe, and its discovery is considered a landmark test of the Big Bang model of the universe.

(1975) AN ARRAY OF TELESCOPES ARE BETTER THAN ONE

Modern computers now permit signals from multiple antennas to be combined to effectively create large apertures for better resolution, as in the **Very Large Array** (VLA). The VLA is a multi-purpose instrument designed to allow investigations of many astronomical objects, including radio galaxies, quasars, pulsars, supernova remnants, gamma ray bursts, radio-emitting stars, the Sun and planets, astrophysical masers and black holes. It also recognizes hydrogen gas that constitutes a large portion of the Milky Way Galaxy as well as external galaxies.

Radio telescopes can produce images of objects in space that would have been missed by an optical telescope. Optical telescopes need to have some kind of light to see an object, but radio telescopes do not need light to "see." The VLA observatory consists of twenty-seven independent antennas, each of which has a dish diameter of twenty-five meters (eighty-two feet) and weighs 230 tons. The telescope race now used instruments weighing hundreds of tons!

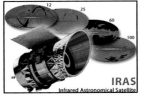

(1983) INFRARED ASTRONOMICAL SATELLITE

IRAS was the first-ever space-based observatory to perform a survey of the entire sky at infrared wavelengths. Launched on January 25, 1983, its mission lasted ten months. The telescope was a joint project of the United States (NASA), the Netherlands (NIVR), and the United Kingdom (SERC). It mapped 96% of the sky four times, at 12, 25, 60, and 100 micrometer wavelengths. It discovered about 350,000 sources, many of which are still awaiting identification. About 75,000 of those are believed to be starburst galaxies still enduring their star-formation stage.

(1986) MIR SOVIET/RUSSIAN SPACE STATION

Mir was a Soviet and later Russian space station, operating in low Earth orbit from 1986 to 2001. Mir served as a microgravity research laboratory in which crews conducted experiments in biology, human biology, physics, astronomy, meteorology, and spacecraft systems in order to develop technologies required for the permanent occupation of space.

The station was the first consistently inhabited long-term research station in space and was operated by a series of long-duration crews. The station was originally launched as part of the Soviet Union's manned spaceflight program effort to maintain a long-term research outpost in space. After the collapse of the USSR, it was operated by the new Russian Federal Space Agency. The cost of the station was estimated to be $4.2 billion over the lifetime of the station.

Mir existed until March 23, 2001, at which point it was deliberately deorbited, and broke apart during atmospheric re-entry.

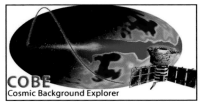

(1989) COSMIC BACKGROUND EXPLORER

The COBE satellite was developed by NASA's Goddard Space Flight Center to measure the diffuse infrared and microwave radiation from the early universe to the limits set by our astrophysical environment.

Its goals were to investigate the cosmic microwave background radiation (CMB) of the universe and provide measurements that would help shape our understanding of the cosmos. This work provided evidence that supported the Big Bang theory of the universe, that the CMB was a near-perfect black-body spectrum and that it had very faint anisotropies.

A team of American scientists announced on April 23, 1992, that they had found the primordial "seeds" (CMBE anisotropy) in data from COBE. The announcement was reported worldwide as a fundamental scientific discovery.

(1990) HUBBLE REVEALS A GRAND CREATION

Since the time of Galileo, astronomers have shared a single goal—to see more, to see further, and to see deeper. In 1946, Lyman Spitzer imagined a national observatory in the sky. Forty-four years later, in April 1990, his imagination became a reality when the **Hubble Space Telescope** was carried into orbit by the space shuttle Discovery. It single-handedly sped humanity to one of its greatest advances in that journey, and to date is widely regarded as the most successful scientific facility in all history.

Hubble is a telescope that orbits Earth. Its position above the atmosphere, which normally distorts and blocks the light that reaches our planet, gives it a view of the universe that far surpasses that of ground-based telescopes. It has beamed hundreds of thousands of images back to Earth, shedding light on many of the great mysteries of astronomy. Enough information to fill about eighteen DVDs is transmitted from Hubble every week. Astronomers can download archived data via the Internet and analyze it from anywhere in the world.

Its gaze has helped determine the age of the universe, the identity of quasars, and the existence of dark energy. When you stitch all the data and images together what has emerged is the Greatest Drama in human history; the creation of an Awe-Inspiring Universe as never before revealed!

Counting all the repairs and fixes since it was put into orbit in 1990, the total cost for the Hubble has been estimated to be about ten billion dollars.

(1991) COMPTON GAMMA RAY OBSERVATORY

The **Compton Gamma Ray Observatory** (CGRO) was a sophisticated satellite observatory dedicated to observing the high-energy Universe. It was the second in NASA's program of orbiting "Great Observatories" following the Hubble Space Telescope. While Hubble's instruments originally operated at visible and ultraviolet wavelengths, Compton carried a collection of four instruments which together could detect an unprecedented broad range of high-energy radiation called *gamma rays*.

Some of its scientific achievements were the discovery of an isotropic distribution of the Gamma-ray burst events, mapping of the Milky Way using the twenty-six Al Gamma-ray line, the discovery of Blazar Active Galactic Nuclei as primary source of the highest energy cosmic Gamma-rays, and the discovery of the "Bursting Pulsar."

At seventeen tons, the Compton was the heaviest astrophysical payload ever flown at the time of its launch on April 5, 1991, aboard the space shuttle Atlantis. Compton was safely de-orbited and re-entered the Earth's atmosphere on June 4, 2000.

(1993-1996) DOUBLE THE SEEING POWER

The **W. M. Keck Observatory** is a two-telescope astronomical observatory at an elevation of 13,600 feet near the summit of Mauna Kea in Hawaii. The primary mirrors of each of the two telescopes are ten meters (thirty-three feet) in diameter, making them (as of 2011) the second largest optical telescopes in the world, slightly smaller than the Gran Telescopio Canarias. The telescopes can operate together to form a single astronomical interferometer.

The weight of each telescope is about 300 tons and the cost in excess of $145 million. Both Keck telescopes are equipped with adaptive optics, which compensates for the blurring due to atmospheric turbulence. The Near Infrared Camera for the Keck I telescope is so sensitive it could detect the equivalent of a single candle flame on the Moon.

(1998) THE VERY LARGE TELESCOPE ARRAY

The **Very Large Telescope** (VLT) is an advanced, ground-based optical instrument, consisting of four Unit Telescopes with main mirrors of 8.2 meters diameter and four movable 1.8 meter diameter auxiliary telescopes. The telescopes can work together, in groups of two or three, to form a giant 'interferometer' allowing astronomers to see details up to twenty-five times finer than with the individual telescopes.

The VLT is a most unusual telescope, based on the latest technology. It is not just one, but an array of four telescopes, each with a main mirror of 8.2 meters in diameter. With one such telescope, images of celestial objects as faint as magnitude 30 have been obtained in a one-hour exposure. This corresponds to seeing objects that are four billion times fainter than those seen with the naked eye.

(1998) INTERNATIONAL SPACE STATION

The **International Space Station** (ISS) is an internationally developed research facility that is being assembled in low Earth orbit. The objective of the ISS, as defined by NASA, is to develop and test technologies for exploration spacecraft systems, develop techniques to maintain crew health and performance on missions beyond low Earth orbit, and gain operational experience that can be applied to exploration missions.

The construction of the station began in 1998 and is scheduled to be completed by mid-2012. It is expected to remain in operation until at least 2015 to possibly 2020. The ISS is the largest artificial satellite that has ever orbited Earth. It serves as a research laboratory that has a microgravity environment in which crews conduct experiments in biology, chemistry, medicine, physiology, and physics, as well as astronomical and meteorological observations. The station provides a unique environment for the testing of the spacecraft systems that will be required for missions to the Moon and Mars.

The station's sections are operated by their builders, the American National Aeronautics and Space Administration (NASA), the European Space Agency (ESA), the Russian Federal Space Agency (RKA), the Japan Aerospace Exploration Agency (JAXA), and the Canadian Space Agency (CSA). The cost of the station has been estimated by ESA as €100 billion over thirty years.

(1999) CHANDRA X-RAY OBSERVATORY

The **Chandra X-Ray Observatory** is a satellite launched by NASA on July 23, 1999. It is a telescope specially designed to detect X-ray emission from very hot regions of the Universe such as exploded stars, clusters of galaxies, and matter around black holes.

Since the Earth's atmosphere absorbs the vast majority of X-rays, and are not detectable from Earth-based telescopes, Chandra must orbit above it, up to an altitude of 139,000 kilometers (86,500 miles) in space. The Smithsonian's Astrophysical Observatory in Cambridge, Massachusetts, hosts the Chandra X-Ray Center which operates the satellite, processes the data, and distributes it to scientists around the world for analysis.

Chandra has imaged the spectacular, glowing remains of exploded stars, and taken spectra showing the dispersal of elements. Chandra has observed the region around the supermassive black hole in the center of our Milky Way, and found black holes across the Universe. Chandra has traced the separation of dark matter from normal matter in the collision of galaxies in a cluster and is contributing to both dark matter and dark energy studies. As its mission continues, Chandra will continue to discover startling new science about our high-energy Universe.

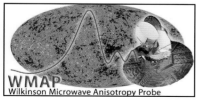

Wilkinson Microwave Anisotropy Probe

(2001) WILKINSON MICROWAVE ANISOTROPY PROBE

WMAP—also known as the Microwave Anisotropy Probe—is a spacecraft which measures the differences in the temperature of the Big Bang's remnant radiant heat—the Cosmic Microwave Background Radiation—across the full sky.

The mission was developed in a joint partnership between the NASA Goddard Space Flight Center and Princeton University. WMAP's measurements played the key role in establishing the current Standard Model of Cosmology. WMAP's data confirms a universe that is dominated by dark energy in the form of a cosmological constant.

Dark energy is a hypothetical form of energy that permeates all of space and tends to increase the rate of expansion of the universe. Dark energy is the most accepted theory to explain recent observations and experiments that the universe appears to be expanding at an accelerating rate. In the standard model of cosmology, dark energy currently accounts for 73% of the total mass-energy of the universe.

(2003) TELESCOPES TO SEE THROUGH STAR DUST

The **Spitzer Space Telescope** is an infrared space observatory launched in 2003. It is the fourth and final of NASA's Great Observatories program—a family of four space-based observatories, each observing the Universe in a different kind of light. The other missions in the program include the visible-light Hubble Space Telescope (HST), Compton Gamma Ray Observatory (CGRO), and the Chandra X-Ray Observatory (CXO).

At the time, Spitzer was the largest infrared telescope ever launched into space. Its highly sensitive instruments allow scientists to peer into cosmic regions that are hidden from optical telescopes, including dusty stellar nurseries, the centers of galaxies, and newly forming planetary systems. Spitzer's infrared eyes also allow astronomers to see cooler objects in space, like failed stars (brown dwarfs), extrasolar planets, giant molecular clouds, and organic molecules that may hold the secret to life on other planets.

The planned mission period was to be two-and-a-half years with a pre-launch expectation that the mission could extend to five or slightly more years until the onboard liquid helium supply was exhausted. This occurred on May 15, 2009. Without liquid helium to cool the telescope to the very cold temperatures needed to operate, most instruments are no longer usable.

(2005) LARGE BINOCULAR TELESCOPE

Located on Mount Graham in southeastern Arizona, the $120 million **Large Binocular Telescope** is a marvel of modern technology with a mass of approximately 580 metric tons. It uses two massive 8.4-meter (27.6 feet) diameter primary mirrors mounted side by side to produce a collecting area equivalent to an 11.8-meter (39 feet) circular aperture. The interferometric combination of the light paths of the two primary mirrors will provide a resolution of a 22.8-meter (seventy-five feet) telescope.

This milestone marks the dawn of a new era in observing the Universe with ground-based telescopes. With unparalleled observational capability, astronomers will be able to view planets in distant solar systems, and detect and measure objects dating back to the beginning of time (fourteen billion years ago). The twin mirrors were polished to an accuracy of 30 nanometers, or 3,000 times thinner than a human hair.

(2007) GRAN TELESCOPIO CANARIAS TELESCOPE

The Gran Telescopio Canarias (GTC) is located on a volcanic peak 7,438 feet above sea level, on the island of La Palma, in the Canary Islands of Spain. It took seven years to construct and cost £112 million ($152 million). Planning for the construction of the telescope, which started in 1987, involved more than one thousand people from one hundred companies.

As of 2011, it is the world's largest single-aperture optical telescope at 10.4 meters with a light-collecting surface of 75.7 square meters. The building that houses the telescope has a height of forty-one meters, six meters less than the Statue of Liberty in New York. The base of the building that holds the dome must withstand a total weight of 500 tons. The 500 tons of telescope, supported on a thin layer of lubricant, can move with a simple push. The GTC is able to study in depth, the nature of black holes, as well as the more distant stars and galaxies in the Universe and the first conditions after the Big Bang. It is expected that the telescope would produce important advances in every field of astrophysics.

(2009) SOUTH POLE TELESCOPE

The **South Pole Telescope** (SPT) is a microwave telescope, measuring 10 meters in diameter, located at the South Pole, Antarctica. The telescope has been in use since February 16, 2007. It is funded by the National Science Foundation. It is a microwave/millimeter-wave telescope that observes in a frequency range between 70 and 300 GHz.

The primary goal of the South Pole Telescope project is to set constraints on the nature of dark energy by measuring its impact on the growth of structure, specifically the formation of the number density of massive galaxy clusters. The South Pole is the premier observing site in the world for millimeter-wavelength observations.

The Pole's high altitude means the atmosphere is thin, and the extreme cold keeps the amount of water vapor in the air low. This is particularly important where incoming signals can be absorbed by water vapor, and where water vapor emits radiation that can be confused with astronomical signals.

(2009) KEPLER SPACE TELESCOPE

The **Kepler Space Telescope** launched on March 7, 2009, is a space observatory designed to discover Earth-like planets orbiting other stars. It will monitor 100,000 main-sequence stars for planets with a mission lifetime of three-and-one-half years extendible to at least six years.

The scientific objective of the Kepler Mission is to explore the structure and diversity of planetary systems. This is achieved by surveying a large sample of stars to: (1) Determine the abundance of terrestrial and larger planets in or near the habitable zone of a wide variety of stars. (2) Determine the distribution of sizes and shapes of the orbits of these planets. (3) Estimate how many planets there are in multiple-star systems. (4) Determine the variety of orbit sizes and planet reflectivity's, sizes, masses, and densities of short-period giant planets. (5) Identify additional members of each discovered planetary system using other techniques. (6) Determine the properties of those stars that harbor planetary systems.

Kepler has found 1,235 planet candidates as of February 2011. The centuries-old quest for other worlds like our Earth has been rejuvenated by the intense excitement and popular interest surrounding the discovery of hundreds of planets orbiting other stars discovered by the Kepler.

(2009) HERSCHEL SPACE OBSERVATORY

Herschel is a European Space Agency (ESA) space observatory sensitive to the far infrared and submillimeter wavebands. At the time of its launch in May 2009, it carried the largest and most powerful infrared telescope (3.5-meter mirror) ever flown in space. A pioneering mission, it is studying the origin and formation of stars and galaxies to help understand how the Universe came to be the way it is today.

Herschel has been designed to observe the "cool universe;" it is observing the structure formation in the early universe revealing galaxy formation at the epochs when most stars in the universe were formed, unveiling the physics and chemistry of the interstellar medium and its molecular clouds, the wombs of the stars, and unraveling the mechanisms governing the formation of stars and their planetary systems, including our own solar system, putting it into context.

(2009) PLANCK SPACE OBSERVATORY

Planck is a space observatory launched in May 2009, designed to observe the anisotropies of the cosmic microwave background (CMB) over the entire sky, using high sensitivity and angular resolution. Planck was created as the third Medium-Sized Mission

(M3) of the European Space Agency's Horizon 2000 Scientific Program. The project, initially called COBRAS/SAMBA, is named in honor of the German physicist Max Planck (1858–1947), who won the Nobel Prize for Physics in 1918.

Planck is expected to yield definitive data on a number of astronomical issues by 2012, and will provide a major source of information relevant to several cosmological and astrophysical issues, such as testing theories of the early universe and the origin of cosmic structure.

(2011) ALPHA MAGNETIC SPECTROMETER

The **Alpha Magnetic Spectrometer (AMS-02)** instrument is a cutting-edge particle physics detector costing two billion dollars. In May 2011 the AMS-02 was attached to the International Space Station (ISS), and is designed to pick up cosmic rays from the Universe as they pass through it. It is expected to test several aspects of theories about the origin and structure of the Universe. It may also reveal the nature of dark matter. Some have expressed that it could reshape modern understandings of the Universe, much the same way that the Hubble Space Telescope pioneered new frontiers in astronomy.

The AMS-02 is to be the first to study charged particles in space. Sam Ting, AMS Principal Investigator from the Massachusetts Institute of Technology was quoted as saying one of his desires is that the particles recorded by AMS-02, prove the existence of a parallel universe made up of anti-matter, or particles that are, in electrical charge and magnetic properties, the exact opposite of regular particles. Such a universe has been theorized but not proven. The discovery of massive amounts of anti-matter could answer fundamental questions about the universe's origin.

The project grew to incorporate more than 500 physicists in some sixteen nations around the world. AMS-02 was mostly built in Europe and Asia. It also received some help from NASA's Johnson Space Center and from the Department of Energy.

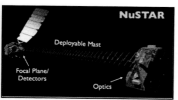

(2012) NUCLEAR SPECTROSCOPIC TELESCOPE ARRAY

The **Nuclear Spectroscopic Telescope Array** (NuSTAR) is an explorer mission that will deploy the first focusing telescopes that will allow astronomers to image and study the Universe in high energy X-rays at 6 to 79 keV from astrophysical sources, especially for nuclear spectroscopy. Our view of the Universe in this spectral window has been limited because previous orbiting telescopes have not employed true focusing optics.

NuSTAR's primary scientific goals are to conduct a deep survey for black holes a billion times more massive than our Sun, understand how particles are accelerated to within a fraction of a percent of the speed of light in active galaxies, and understand how the elements are created in the explosions of massive stars by imaging the remains, which are called supernova remnants. NASA has contracted with Orbital Sciences Corporation to launch NuSTAR on a Pegasus XL rocket on February 3, 2012.

(2013) ATACAMA LARGE MILLIMETER ARRAY

Atacama Large Millimeter Array (ALMA), a state-of-the-art telescope, is designed to study light from some of the coldest objects in the Universe. This light has wavelengths of around a millimeter, between infrared light and radio waves, and is therefore known as millimeter and sub-millimeter radiation. ALMA is the most powerful telescope for observing the cool Universe—molecular gas and dust, as well as the relic radiation of the Big Bang. ALMA will study the building blocks of stars, planetary systems, galaxies, and life itself. ALMA's main array will have fifty twelve-meter antennas, arranged in configurations spread over distances from 150 meters to sixteen kilometers. And just when you thought telescopes could not get any heaver, they did, with each weighing over 100 tons (over 5,000 tons in total). The total cost estimated to be more than a billion dollars. The array will thus simulate a single, giant telescope much larger than any that could actually be built. The ALMA project is an international collaboration between Europe, East Asia, and North America in cooperation with the Republic of Chile. The ability to reposition its antennas is part of what makes ALMA such a powerful telescope.

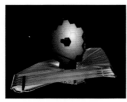

(2015) JAMES WEBB TELESCOPE

When the Webb telescope is launched in 2015 it will be the successor to the Hubble telescope and will be the premier observatory of the next decade. The JWST or Webb Telescope's main scientific goal is to observe the most distant objects in the universe beyond the reach of either ground-based instruments or the Hubble. It will study every phase in the history of our Universe, ranging from the first luminous glows after the Big Bang, to the formation of solar systems capable of supporting life on planets like Earth, to the formation of our own Solar System. Its projected cost is $6.5 billion and rising.

Webb will look at the Universe primarily by infrared, while Hubble studies it primarily at optical and ultraviolet wavelengths (though it has some infrared capability). Webb also has a much bigger mirror than Hubble. This larger light-collecting area means that Webb can peer farther back into time than Hubble is capable of doing. Hubble is in a very close orbit around the Earth, while the JWST will orbit the Sun approximately 1,500,000 kilometers (930,000 miles) on the far side of Earth at the L2 Lagrange point.

(2018) GIANT MAGELLAN TELESCOPE

The Giant Magellan Telescope (GMT) will be a product of more than a century of astronomical research and telescope building by some of the world's leading research institutions. It will open a new window on the universe for the twenty-first century.

Scheduled for completion around 2018, the GMT will consist of seven 8.4-meter mirror segments that will be arranged to form a single optical surface having the resolving power of a 24.5-meter (80 feet) primary mirror. It will open new avenues of scientific exploration, including understanding the origin and formation of planetary systems, witnessing the formation of stars, galaxies, and black holes, exploring the properties of dark matter and dark energy in the cosmos, and Detecting First Light and the Reionization of the Universe.

As has been the case with all new telescopes, the GMT's unanticipated discoveries will open frontiers previously unexpected and unimagined, providing new windows onto the cosmos. (*Image credit: Giant Magellan Telescope-GTMO Cooperation*)

(2018) THIRTY METER TELESCOPE

The Thirty Meter Telescope (TMT) is a planned ground-based astronomical observatory with a thirty-meter (ninety-eight-foot) diameter segmented mirror that consist of 492 individual 1.45-meter mirror segments capable of observations from the near-ultraviolet to the mid-infrared.

An adaptive optics system will correct for image blur caused by the atmosphere of the Earth. At wavelengths longer than 0.8 μm, this correction will enable observations with ten times the spatial resolution of the Hubble Space Telescope. TMT will be the first of the new generation of Extremely Large Telescopes. The telescope cost was estimated in 2009 to be $970 million to $1.2 billion.

With the TMT, astronomers will be able to locate and analyze the light from the first stellar systems born soon after the Big Bang, determine the physical processes governing the formation of galaxies like our own Milky Way, study planet formation around nearby stars, and make observations that test the fundamental laws of physics. However, it is the unexpected discoveries that TMT will make that will likely be the most exciting.

(2018) EUROPEAN EXTREMELY LARGE TELESCOPE

Just when you think telescopes can't possibly get any larger, they will in 2018. The European Extremely Large Telescope (E-ELT) will be a ground-based astronomical observatory with a **42-meter** (138 feet) diameter segmented mirror. The telescope's "eye" will be almost half the length of a football pitch in diameter and will gather fifteen times more light than the largest optical telescopes operating today with an estimated cost of well over $1 billion.

The telescope has an innovative five-mirror design that includes advanced adaptive optics to correct for the turbulent atmosphere, giving exceptional image quality. The E-ELT will gather 100,000,000 times more light than the human eye, 8,000,000 times more than Galileo's telescope, and twenty-six times more than a single VLT Unit Telescope. In fact, the E-ELT will gather more light than all of the existing 8- to10-meter class telescopes on the planet combined.

The E-ELT is a revolutionary new ground-based telescope concept, with a performance that is orders of magnitude better than currently existing facilities. Such a telescope may, eventually, revolutionize our perception of the Universe, much as Galileo's telescope did 400 years ago.

(2019) OVERWHELMINGLY LARGE TELESCOPE

The Overwhelmingly Large Telescope (OWL) is a conceptual design by the European Southern Observatory (ESO) organization for an extremely large telescope, which was intended to have a single aperture of one hundred meters in diameter. Because of the complexity and the $1.6 billion cost of building a telescope of this unprecedented size, ESO has elected to focus on the 42-meter diameter European Extremely Large Telescope instead.

The OWL could have been expected to regularly see astronomical objects with an apparent magnitude of thirty-eight or 1,500 times fainter than the faintest object which has been detected by the Hubble Space Telescope. Experience gained in existing segmented mirrors suggests that the 100-meter mirror proposed for the OWL is feasible and may very well be built sometime in the future. With this ambitious design, ESO proves that man's imagination is trumped only by the depth of his pockets.

Types of Telescopes In Use Today

Cosmic-ray	Optical reflecting	Space
Gamma-ray	Optical refactoring	Submillimeter
Gravitational wave	Radio	Ultraviolet
High Energy Particle	Solar	X-ray
Infrared		

No Limits to Man's Quest or Imagination

As seen from this brief history of the development of the telescope there appears to be no end in sight for man's obsessive quest to the stars, or limits to his imagination to devise new ways to have a closer look at the incredible Universe.

Even as the next generation of telescopes is being readied for first light, there are new ideas on the drawing boards that will make the latest technology seem old school. Time and time again, each generation of telescope builders have outdone those before them, resulting in discovering even more incredible secrets of the Universe. This, in turn, drives their passion of discovery to an even higher pitch.

Those things now unknown to us that will be discovered with the emerging technologies will inspire our imaginations in the future to even greater heights than we thought possible. This will inevitably draw us in deeper to this unquenchable thirst for greater knowledge of the stars. There appears to be no turning back now in man's cosmic obsession as he is compelled forward in his endeavor to search for answers.

Man's quest has even taken him underground with particle accelerators like the Large Hadron Collider (LHC) in search of the Higgs boson, often referred to as "the God particle" by the media. The existence of the particle is postulated to resolve inconsistencies in theoretical physics. The LHC was built in collaboration with over 10,000 scientists and engineers from over 100 countries, as well as hundreds of universities and laboratories. It is one of the most expensive scientific instruments ever built at a cost of between six to ten billion dollars by best estimates.

If Galileo could only see the Insatiable Quest his imagination fueled with the use of that simple telescope 400 years ago. He would observe how each generation after him raced to improve upon their view of the Universe as they were drawn toward it like metal to a magnet. Or if Isaiah could only see the reality of what you and I are now privileged to see through the eye of the Hubble telescope. They would see themselves as characters among a string of cast members performing their part to bring to humankind the Grandest Drama in history. A drama that takes us to the core of our very existence!

What awaits us to be revealed as the next generation of telescopes comes on line in the very near future? No one can really say for sure, but it will likely be beyond anything we could have imagined based on our experience thus far.

After this brief review of man's journey with the invention of the telescope, would you agree that man truly has been embarked on an insatiable quest to the stars? As you will learn on the pages just ahead, you will see that the money and time spent on this quest have not been in vain. You will see revealed the unfathomable truth in the words spoken by Isaiah.

Man's Quest to Know and Understand Takes On New Dimensions

For MILLENNIA, CURIOSITY has driven man to explore the world around him. This is how humans grow and progress as a society. Through the study of plant life on Earth, man has come to realize the importance of photosynthesis and how it is arguably the most important biological process on Earth.

Through his studies, man has come to realize that marine life represents a vast resource, providing food, medicine, and raw materials. He now knows that marine organisms contribute significantly to the oxygen cycle and are involved in the regulation of the Earth's climate. He also understands the need to maintain a proper balance.

Through the study of birds and animals, many of man's inventions have come into existence. Biomimicry, or looking to nature for design inspiration, is not new; its guiding principles have served to inspire architectural works, aviation breakthroughs, designs in robotics, and a host of other inventions.

Now, with the invention of flying telescopes placed in orbit above the Earth's atmosphere for clearer visibility, man has a new world of discovery open to him. A world unlike anything he has ever explored or studied here on Earth. This world is one that was perhaps best described in an article that appeared in *National Geographic* a few decades ago under the heading "The Incredible Universe:"

> *Far From The Land of everyday, out in the distant curves of the universe lie strange and fantastic realms, unlike anything in our wildest dreams. Hidden by the barriers of time and space, they have lived forever beyond the reach of man, unknown and unexplored. But now, just now the cosmic barriers have begun to lift a little. Man has had his first glimpses of these once-secret domains, and their bizarre ways have left him stunned. They challenge his very notion of matter and energy. With Alice in Wonderland, he says, "One can't believe impossible things." And impossible, indeed they seem to be.*

> *In those far reaches of the universe, in those bewildering worlds, are places . . . Where a teaspoon of matter weighs as much as 200 million elephants . . . Where a tiny whirling star winks on and off thirty times a second . . . Where a small mysterious object shines with the brilliance of ten trillion suns . . . Where matter and light are continually sucked up by devouring black holes, never to be seen again.*

It is as if many of the inventions man has devised over the millenniums have led us to this point of discovery as though being drawn by an invisible force much like that of a magnet. As we look out upon this world, it forces us to see that we are a small but important part of a much bigger picture. This is a world our forefathers knew nothing of, even though they, too, had been drawn along in the quest to know and understand why we are here and what our purpose is.

This new world is so immense we can only measure its distance in light-years. (A light-year is the distance light travels in a year at the speed of 186,282 miles a second, which is equivalent to six trillion miles.) To put it into perspective, think of the Earth as a speck of dust, then place that speck of dust onto a grain of sand, which would represent our Sun; then place that grain of sand onto a dime, which would represent our Milky Way galaxy; and then place that dime onto the Earth, which would represent the known universe.

When we look in perspective at our place in the universe, the Earth appears to be but a speck of dust. Yet, here we are, on this planet, which to man seemed bigger than life until he discovered this Doorway that has revealed a world far beyond anything he could ever have imagined. As we look upon this new world, it becomes stunningly clear that it is not of man's making. Yet, we have been privileged as pioneers to be the first to discover it through the use of our imagination. It will be up to future generations to build on our knowledge and use their own imaginations to take additional materials from the Earth to sculpt and devise a means to travel through that Doorway to explore a strange new world unexplored up to the present.

As we make our way through this Doorway and ascend higher for a closer look, it becomes inescapably clear that this incredible world beyond our sky could not have been created without imagination. Could we, would we, deny that all the incredible things man has created and devised up until now came about randomly and devoid of imagination? Common logic leads you to believe that Supreme Imagination was at work when you examine the precise and orderly design of it all.

The invitation extended to us twenty-seven hundred years ago has now taken on an incredible dimension as a result of flying space telescopes. As the Grand Drama unfolds before you in the pages ahead, take time to look at the detail of the Hubble images that show multitudes of spiral galaxies in the background. Meditate upon what must have gone into their design—with each having billions of stars like ours, and no doubt trillions of planets. Ponder how thrilling it would be to explore them one day in the future! The knowledge we have gained or ever will gain here on Earth pales in comparison to what awaits us just ahead in this Awe-Inspiring Universe!

"That deep emotional conviction of the presence of a Superior reasoning power, which is revealed in the incomprehensible universe, forms my idea of God." Albert Einstein

ACT IV

A GRAND ARCHITECT IS REVEALED

RESULTING FROM 400 YEARS OF MAN'S IMAGINATION

Hubble in orbit, 353 miles above Earth, peering into the universe.

IMAGINATION OF MAN

Gazing Into Our Universe: Peering Into a Mind of Supreme Imagination

The Hubble, as it has become known, has opened up a whole new frontier of discoveries in the heavens. It is as though we have been given a peek into the mind of Imagination Supreme. We have discovered wonderful things, yet they are so vast and complex that it is difficult for the human mind to comprehend. According to NASA:

Hubble's discoveries have transformed the way scientists look at the universe. It has beamed hundreds of thousands of images back to Earth, shedding light on many of the great mysteries of astronomy. Its gaze has helped determine the age of the universe, the identity of quasars, and the existence of dark energy. Its ability to show the universe in unprecedented detail has turned astronomical conjectures into concrete certainties. It has winnowed down the collection of theories about the universe even as it sparked new ones, clarifying the path for future astronomers.

The universe we can see with the naked eye is only a tiny fraction of the universe that exists. With the invention of telescopes, and through the use of his imagination, man has discovered a world far beyond his own comprehension. This is a world where time seems endless and dimension and space have no boundaries. A world where an unexplainable energy seems to be emitting from every direction, and a universe so impossible to conceptualize that it staggers human imagination, a universe so vast that it makes our solar system as insignificant as a single grain of sand on the seashore!

When we look at the awe-inspiring photos taken by the Hubble, Spitzer, and other space telescopes, it looks as if these scenes were meticulously painted by brush onto a black-velvet canvas by a Great Artist with imagination without compare. The reality is that they are not mere paintings by mortals; but a living orchestra of heavenly bodies playing in concert, millions of light-years away, on a scale incomprehensible to the imagination of man.

With the invention of space telescopes orbiting above the Earth, man has been elevated closer to the heavens to peer deep into space. It is as though he had been invited to a Grand Premier of Creation itself, where only those who understand its significance, find themselves in Awe of its Supreme Majesty.

One has to wonder why we, of all generations, have been given this awe-inspiring glimpse into Supreme Imagination. Could it be that man, unbeknownst to himself, is merely responding to a Divine Invitation?

"Look up into the heavens. Who created all the stars?"

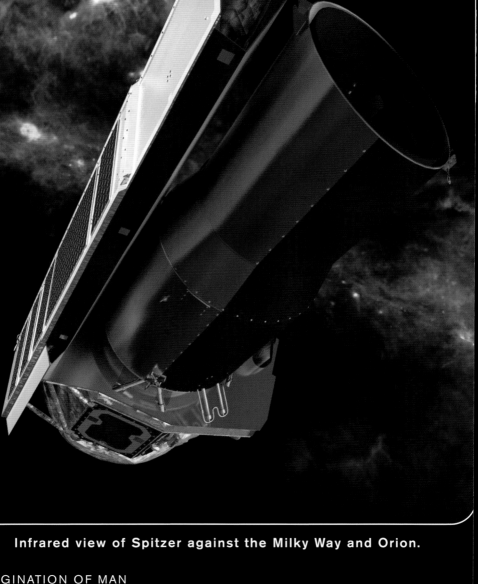

Infrared view of Spitzer against the Milky Way and Orion.

IMAGINATION OF MAN

Unveiling Long-Hidden Secrets of the Universe

For millennia, man has gazed at the night sky in hopes of unveiling its secrets and revealing the mysteries about how it came about and what the meaning of it all is. Until this generation, man's sight into the vast unknown has been limited by the Earth's atmosphere, which was like a veil that distorted our view of distant worlds far beyond our reach. In 1990, the Hubble telescope began to orbit above Earth's atmosphere. It could now peer out into the universe without a subject-distorting veil. Man had now achieved a major breakthrough in unveiling the secrets of those distant worlds. But, even in deep space, there are things still kept from Hubble's gaze. Many regions of space are filled with vast dense clouds of gas and dust, which block the view and remain hidden from optical telescopes.

The Spitzer is an infrared cousin of the Hubble Space Telescope that followed Hubble into space in 2003. Its mission was to study stars, galaxies, and planetary disks. Spitzer detects infrared—longer wavelength—light that our eyes cannot see. It detects the infrared energy, or heat, radiated by objects in space and is able to detect dust disks around stars. This is considered an important signpost of planetary formation.

It allowed the observatory back here on Earth to see through the dust by delivering light to advanced, large-format, infrared detector arrays. At the time of its launch, Spitzer was the largest infrared telescope ever launched into space. Its highly sensitive instruments gave us a unique view of the universe and allow us to peer into regions of space which are hidden from optical telescopes.

> *According to NASA "the Spitzer mission is the fourth and final observatory under NASA's Great Observatories program, which also includes the Hubble Space Telescope, Chandra X-Ray Observatory, and Compton Gamma Ray Observatory. It is also the first new mission under NASA's Origins program, which seeks to answer the questions: "Where did we come from?" "Are we alone?"*

Once hidden secrets about the universe are slowly being revealed as man, through his imagination, advances space-telescope technology to the edge. Man has long harbored a burning desire to know where he came from, and if he is alone. This is driving the human imagination to do what mere years ago seemed completely unheard of— even impossible. This tells us that the impossible is, after all, possible. No generations before us have witnessed such spectacular views of the universe. We can give thanks to the collective imaginations of those who pioneered the way for NASA, and the far-sighted individuals who helped create the Hubble and Spitzer telescopes that have given us front-row seats to marvel at an unfolding drama without parallel.

Since biblical times people have put their trust in the Genesis account of creation. In recent years however, their faith has been challenged by some modern-day scientists that say there is no scientific evidence to support Genesis. As you will learn from recent discoveries, the idea of no scientific evidence to support Genesis is now being turned upside down by the very findings of NASA's Hubble and Spitzer telescopes.

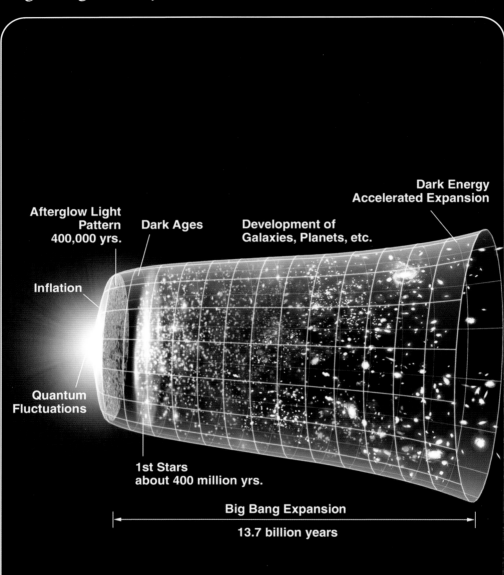

Man imagines how the universe began.

Man Imagines How The Universe Began

How did our universe begin? This seminal question has been pondered by man since the dawn of time. Do we finally have the answers, now that we can peer back into time with sophisticated space telescopes? Have we been led to this point in history by a higher power that wants to reveal this Grand Architect to us? The plot thickens!

There are no irrefutable answers to these questions yet, but what we do know is that this is the most exciting time in man's history. With newfound technology, today's astronomers are like kids on the loose at Disney World for the first time. There are so many thrilling things to see and take in that they find themselves ecstatic and in awe of it all. The stunning revelations now being made have only added fuel to man's insatiable quest for more knowledge. Already better and far more powerful telescopes, like the **Next Generation Space Telescope (NGST)** are in the pipeline to replace the Hubble and Spitzer when they go out of service. See http://www.jwst.nasa.gov/firstlight.html for more details. Notice what NASA states about the James Webb Space Telescope under the heading The End of the Dark Ages: First Light and Reionization:

> *Until around 400 million years after the Big Bang, the Universe was a very dark place. There were no stars, and there were no galaxies. Scientists would like to unravel the story of exactly what happened after the Big Bang. The James Webb Space Telescope will pierce this veil of mystery and reveal the story of the formation of the first stars and galaxies in the Universe.*

The Big Bang theory is the latest in man's imagining how the universe began. The essential idea behind the theory is that the universe began and has expanded from a primordial, extremely hot and dense initial condition at some finite time in the past and continues to expand to this day, indicating the beginning of a never-ending universe. Will this theory pan out or will it be replaced by an even more accurate account, based on further research and investigation? Only time will tell. Remember that, based on their limited information, people in the classical era believed the Earth was flat. Through study and investigation, man later realized that it was spherical. Nevertheless, even that was not proved beyond a shadow of a doubt until much later in history. In 1959, Yuri Gagarin became the first human to view Earth from space, where he declared: *"I can see Earth in the view port of the Vzor."* He was followed by the crew of Apollo 8 in 1968. And, then, in 1972, the crew of Apollo 17 captured the famous "Blue Marble" photo of the planet Earth, and saw for a certainty that it was spherical and hanging upon nothing, just as the early Biblical writings had stated.

Our true understanding about how the universe began and where we are headed seems to be limited by the knowledge that we have collected from the creative imaginations of those who lived before us. This legacy is combined with our own imaginations in devising new ways to explore the universe around us to take us ever closer to the heavens. Consider this important question: *Could it be that we are overlooking the greatest source of knowledge that has ever existed, a source with a mind and Imagination beyond human comprehension?*

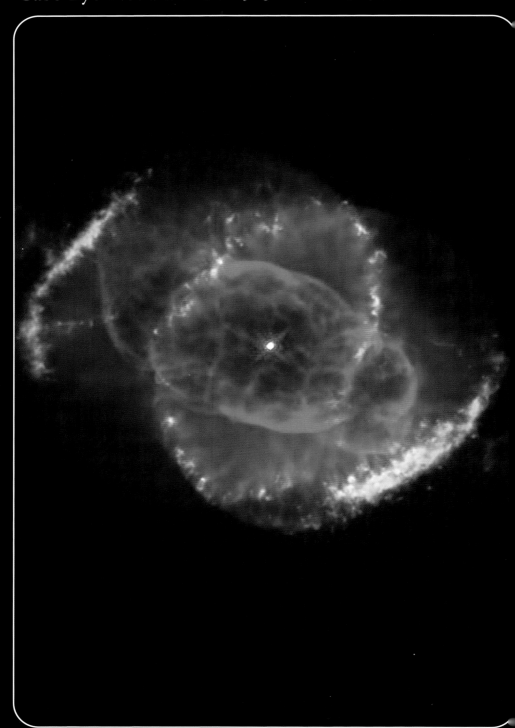

Intricate Structure in the Universe

As man explores the universe with Hubble, Spitzer, and other space telescopes, it becomes apparent that there is order in the design of the universe and evidence of a Grand Designer. But, when some look at the Big Bang theory, they may wonder, "How can you get orderly design out of an immense explosion of energy?" Have you ever been to a fireworks display? What did you see? You saw an explosion of raw energy in the form of gunpowder, yet it resulted in a beautiful organized display of color and design. Fireworks (devices) take many forms to produce the four primary effects: noise, light, smoke, and floating materials.

Fireworks were originally invented by the Chinese for entertainment purposes. This was a natural extension of the Chinese invention of gunpowder. In China, they were first made by fireworks masters who were well-respected for their knowledge of the many complex techniques used to create truly dazzling fireworks displays. Yes, complex techniques required by skilled craftsmen are necessary to create the right effects, not just some gunpowder packed into a rocket and exploded. For example, pyrotechnic compounds are required to produce specific colors and effects such as the Peony, Chrysanthemum, Dahlia, Roman Candle, Palm, Horsetail, Spider, Fish, and many others.

If the beginning of the Universe began with a big bang of energy, as the theory suggests, it was not a disorganized explosion like a keg of gunpowder exploding on a universal scale. Hubble and Spitzer now reveal that there is order in the universe, although it appears it emanated from an explosive beginning, much like a beautiful exploding fireworks display. It appears to have been controlled and organized by technical and creative design. This is what NASA had to say about the Cat's Eye Nebula:

This NASA Hubble Space Telescope image shows one of the most complex planetary nebulae ever seen, NGC 6543, nicknamed the "Cat's Eye Nebula." Hubble reveals surprisingly intricate structures including concentric gas shells, jets of high-speed gas and unusual shock-induced knots of gas.

We are now witnessing, for the first time in human history, as a result of high-powered space telescopes, an explosive display of beautiful design that gives astronomers the same thrill they must have received when they witnessed their first fireworks display as a child. No—we do not fully understand how the universe came about any more than a child fully knows the inner workings of fireworks. When we see the images delivered to us from space and the variety of galaxies, stars, nebula, quasars, neutron stars, black holes, supernovas, and other cosmic effects, we can only imagine that these creative displays of energy were conceived and prepared by a Superior Craftsman and not just some random event.

It seems His intent was to impress us with a dazzling technical fireworks display on a universal scale without compare.

SUPREME IMAGINATION

Power and Energy Beyond Our Comprehension

The ancient writings that invite us to look up into the heavens and see their splendor confidently state that not one of them is missing. Yes, each heavenly body (numbered in the billions of *trillions*) is named and accounted for. Then, the writer poses the question *"Who created all the stars?"* Like any great artist, the Creator of these heavenly bodies must know His own works of art, each one a masterpiece.

How can we resist the invitation to look up into the heavens when we behold cosmic displays like this? This awe-inspiring image, taken with NASA's Hubble Telescope, depicts bright-blue, newly formed stars that are blowing a cavity in the center of a star-forming region in the Small Magellanic Cloud in the constellation Tucana, roughly 200,000 light-years from the Earth. Notice what NASA had to say about The Small Magellanic Cloud:

> *Dwarf galaxies such as the Small Magellanic Cloud, with significantly fewer stars compared to our own galaxy, are considered to be the primitive building blocks of larger galaxies. The study of star formation within this dwarf galaxy is particularly interesting to astronomers because its primitive nature means that it lacks a large percentage of the heavier elements that are forged in successive generations of stars through nuclear fusion.*

Is it not interesting that those ancient writings also state that *"He brings forth the army of them by his great power and incomparable strength?"* Yes. The Architect of such powerful and dynamic stars and galaxies in the universe would have to possess power and energy beyond human imagination. Consider the makeup of these heavenly bodies, such as our Sun, with a core temperature of twenty-seven million degrees Fahrenheit. According to the Big Bang theory, the compact core temperature of the universe at its conception was 1,800 trillion trillion degrees Fahrenheit, during the so-called Planck time.

While scientists often disagree on how the universe came into being, do you not find it interesting that they all agree that its source is a source of incomparable energy beyond human comprehension? Also interesting is that scientists have now discovered an unexplainable force they call **Dark Energy** that is changing our universe, forcing galaxies apart, faster and faster. For more information on dark energy, you can go to Hubble's website at: http://hubblesite.org/hubble_discoveries/darkenergy/

Look at this image of the Small Magellanic Cloud or go to the Hubble website at: http://hubblesite.org/newcenter/archive/releases/2007/04/image/a/ and notice all the spiral galaxies in the background. Just imagine what this image represents and the imagination, design, laws of physics, thermodynamics, gravity, and a whole host of other forces that went into their intricate design.

Blueprints to a Grand Architecture Discovered

Considering that this Grand Architecture just now coming to light was billions of years in the making, it makes one wonder what Supreme Imagination was used to conceive and create such an undertaking. We can only stand in awe when we consider The Mind behind the Universe.

If man, with his creative imagination, has conceived all the things that he has developed from his beginning on this planet, including trying to shape and improve the world and the manufacture of flying telescopes to circle the Earth to peer out into the vast Universe—is it such a stretch for us to imagine that our Grand Universe and our home, the Earth, and life itself, were conceived and created by Someone with a Superior Imagination?

Notice what NASA had to say about the V838 Monocerotis Light Echo:

> **Starry Night,** *Vincent van Gogh's famous painting, is renowned for its bold whorls of light sweeping across a raging night sky. Although this image of the heavens came only from the artist's restless imagination, a new picture from NASA's Hubble Space Telescope bears remarkable similarities to the van Gogh work, complete with never-before-seen spirals of dust swirling across trillions of miles of interstellar space.*
>
> *This image, obtained with the Advanced Camera for Surveys on February 8, 2004, is Hubble's latest view of an expanding halo of light around a distant star, named V838 Monocerotis (V838 Mon). The illumination of interstellar dust comes from the red supergiant star at the middle of the image, which gave off a flashbulb-like pulse of light two years ago. V838 Mon is located about 20,000 light-years away from Earth in the direction of the constellation Monoceros, placing the star at the outer edge of our Milky Way galaxy.*

If Vincent van Gogh's imagination is responsible for the painting *Starry Night,* then what inspired him? Could it have been the mesmerizing grandeur of the night sky? Think of the imagination that went into this Heavenly Masterpiece called Monocerotis Light Echo!

It is as if Hubble and Spitzer have stumbled upon the blueprints of Heaven and Earth. New prints and discoveries, like the V838 Monocerotis Light Echo, are being uncovered every day and transmitted back to Earth to be pored over to glean every detail of this Grand Architecture. The universe is being revealed one frame at a time, as if it was recorded for us long ago as a testament to the imagination responsible for all these incredible things.

The paintings of van Gogh, Monet, and the most accomplished human artists to ever have lived pale in comparison to this grand work of living art captured by the eye of the Hubble telescope in January 2002.

A Massive Cosmic Vineyard Spreads Out Into Infinity

From an early time, our universe took on a majestic appearance. Spun from an incomprehensible source of matter, light, and energy, it has grown like a massive cosmic vineyard as it spread out into infinity. With its roots firmly planted, it has budded and blossomed forth, stars without number, collecting in massive black holes to become the central powerhouse for galaxies that, in turn, have given birth to billions of other stars, that, in turn, have birthed planets and other cosmic phenomenon.

As its cosmic vines sprawled out, the Universe has produced a kaleidoscope of cosmic nebula, like exploding fireworks displays, as if painted with colorful cosmic dust. These nebulas are like masterpieces of art displayed in a cosmic gallery throughout the heavens. Its billions of galaxies have formed into galaxy clusters, like grapes on a vine, with each galaxy displaying its own personality, beauty, and intrigue.

Is it not interesting that from one tiny grape seed nurtured over time, you can grow a massive vineyard that covers an entire continent with grape clusters as far as the eye can see? What a miracle of life wrapped up in such a tiny seed! Could this same miracle of the creative process shed light on how our Grand Universe formed, expanded, and spread out over billions of years like a colossal vineyard? Has it been feeding upon dark matter and energy? The clusters of galaxies exist as far as man's space telescopes can see. A NASA news release (November 2, 2005) discussed our early universe:

Scientists See Light that May Be from First Objects in Universe

Scientists using NASA's Spitzer Space Telescope say they have detected light that may be from the earliest objects in the universe. If confirmed, the observation provides a glimpse of an era more than 13 billion years ago when, after the fading embers of the theorized Big Bang gave way to millions of years of pervasive darkness, the universe came alive. This artist's concept shows what the very early universe might have looked like, just after its first stars began bursting onto the scene. This light could be from the very first stars or perhaps from hot gas falling into the first black holes . . . Scientists theorize that almost instantaneously after the Big Bang, matter began clumping together due to quantum fluctuations. Gravity kicked in next, causing those clumps to grow into larger clouds of invisible hydrogen gas (colored blue here). Eventually, around 200 to 400 million years after the Big Bang, the gas ignited and stars were born.

Is it possible that the stars in the Universe are feeding upon the soil of dark energy as the Universe expands outward from its small but powerful seed of origin? Like a vineyard that feeds upon its field of rich soil, the universe continues to expand exponentially at an accelerated rate the older it becomes. Perhaps we will never fully understand how the universe was formed, but isn't it wonderful that we now have discovered a Doorway to the universe to help us in our quest to know?

A Mere Reflection of the Reality

Take a good look at the Hubble Ultra Deep Field photo taken by the Hubble Space Telescope and think about what the reality of this image represents. This picture is an image of a tiny core sample of space, viewing as many as 10,000 or more galaxies with each containing billions of stars. Notice what NASA says about the image:

> *Galaxies, galaxies everywhere—as far as NASA's Hubble Space Telescope can see. This view of nearly 10,000 galaxies is the deepest visible-light image of the cosmos. Called the Hubble Ultra Deep Field, this galaxy-studded view represents a "deep" core sample of the universe, cutting across billions of light-years. Peering into the Ultra Deep Field is like looking through an eight-foot-long soda straw.*

Believe it or not, this single photo (each point of light represents a galaxy) is the culmination of 400 years of man's imagination, insatiable quest, determination, blood, sweat, and tears, as well as billions of dollars to capture it. Consider for a moment all that went into capturing this fuzzy yet magnificent image.

To plumb the genesis of man's romance with space, we must first go back over 400 years, to when the telescope was invented in the seventeenth century. This marked, in earnest, the start of man's desire to explore space, coincident with the study of astronomy. It would require the discovery of gravity by Sir Isaac Newton and relativity by Albert Einstein. Next, it would require the invention of electricity, radio transmission, manned air flight, rocket propulsion, computers, digital photography, the space shuttle (considered by some to be the most complex machine ever devised by man), and the Hubble space telescope; plus millions of man hours, billions of dollars, and a host of other inventions. Then, finally, 800 separate exposures of the coin-size area in space.

Consider this photo is only a mere image of the reality. If it took all that human imagination, thought, study, and centuries of effort to create a single photo image of a tiny portion of the universe, then what is to be said about the imagination and effort that went into the creation of the universe itself? Like a Grand Conductor, conducting a harmonious orchestra, it appears that the Architect of the heavens intends to impress upon us the superior wisdom and power he possessed as the Grand Conductor of the Universe, and to demonstrate the impossibility of man to control or govern the heavens.

The reality could only come from billions of years of imagination, thought, and effort on the part of One with a mind of Superior Imagination. For one to imagine that the Universe came about by chance without a Superior Designer would be like imagining that the Hubble space telescope came about on its own, without a designer. It just happened to be orbiting the Earth, taking photo images of the Universe without man's imagination or effort. It just happened to take 800 photos of the same spot in space in 400 orbits around Earth from September 24, 2003, and January 16, 2004, to deliver such a magnificent photo. Who would be foolish enough to believe such a story? Could you convince NASA that Hubble was just a random object that just happened along without their creative genius?

SUPREME IMAGINATION

Where Does Light and Darkness Come From?

When Galileo peered up at the heavens, he could only see a tiny fraction of what we now see with the aid of sophisticated telescopes. With space telescopes, man has discovered that there is much more light and darkness out there than the Sun and night sky than Galileo was able to observe with his primitive telescope. But even the most powerful telescopes cannot see to the end of darkness as they peer out quadrillions upon quadrillions of miles into space.

Our Sun, with a core temperature of twenty-seven million degrees, has a mass of about 333,000 times the Earth's. The Sun is 1,391,000 kilometers (862,400 miles) in diameter, Earth is 12,742 kilometers (7,900 miles) in diameter, yet our Sun is only one of perhaps 400 billion other stars in our Milky Way galaxy, a tiny speck among the billions of *trillions* of other stars in the universe. Just consider the light produced by the Sombrero Galaxy. It is thought to be some 50,000 light-years across (about half the diameter of our Milky Way galaxy), yet containing some 800 billion stars. Astronomers think outer material may be falling into a compact core that suggests there may be a super-massive black hole weighing as much as a billion stars at the heart of it. Notice what NASA had to say about this galaxy:

> *NASA's Hubble Space Telescope has trained its razor-sharp eye on one of the universe's most stately and photogenic galaxies, the Sombrero galaxy, Messier 104 (M104). The galaxy's hallmark is a brilliant-white bulbous core encircled by the thick dust lanes comprising the spiral structure of the galaxy. As seen from Earth, the galaxy is tilted nearly edge-on. We view it from just six degrees north of its equatorial plane. This brilliant galaxy was named the Sombrero because of its resemblance to the broad rim and high-topped Mexican hat.*

When you consider that the Sombrero Galaxy is only one of more than one hundred billion other galaxies in the known universe, does it not cause you to ponder the question "Where does light come from?" Galileo could never have known that there was so much more to learn and behold beyond his view of the night sky and the brilliance of our distant Sun!

As we ponder the source of light and darkness, we have to stand in awe of the Imagination and dynamic power behind such incredible bodies of light. We have to wonder how much more lies beyond our present vision of the Universe. How much more will future generations, with ever more sophisticated equipment, be privileged to see and perhaps, one day, explore? The question "Where does light come from?" is, in and of itself, a much more complex question than we might initially conceive. Who can comprehend the answer, let alone the imagination and power that went into its creation?

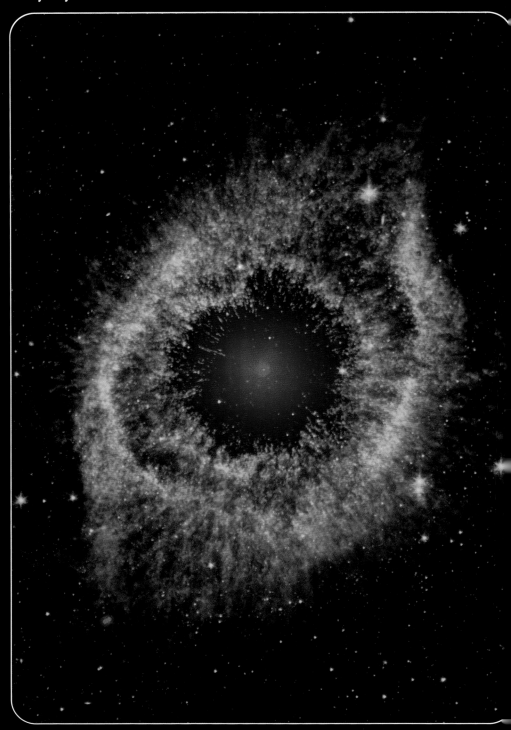

SUPREME IMAGINATION

A Grand Masterpiece on Display

You have heard of Picasso. You may have seen the work of Monet or the master-pieces painted by Leonardo da Vinci—but have you ever come across a master work of art like the Dusty Eye of the Helix Nebula on a galactic scale with the Universe as its canvas?

The Grand Artist who created this masterpiece no doubt used His imagination, much like Picasso, Monet, and da Vinci used theirs; but instead of painting on a cloth canvas with colored oil paints, he used gaseous layers that are heated by the hot core of a dead star, called a "white dwarf," that shine with infrared and visible colors, along with a cosmic dust storm, and emit incredible amounts of energy—as hot as 200,000 degrees Fahrenheit. He used the Universe as His black backdrop, as if it were sprinkled with luminous stardust.

This Grand Work of art could not be measured against that of mere mortals, especially when you consider that the gallery that has acquired this exquisite work is 700 light-years away in the constellation Aquarius and belongs to a class of objects called "planetary nebula." This piece is known by the locals as the eye of the green monster. NASA press release, February 12, 2007:

Comets Clash at Heart of Helix Nebula

A bunch of rowdy comets are colliding and kicking up dust around a dead star, according to new observations from NASA's Spitzer Space Telescope. The dead star lies at the center of the much-photographed Helix Nebula, a shimmering cloud of gas with an eerie resemblance to a giant eye. "We were surprised to see so much dust around this star," noted one professor of the University of Arizona. "The dust must be coming from comets that survived the death of their sun." Spitzer's spectacular new view of the Helix Nebula shows colors as seen in infrared. The dusty dead star appears as a dot in the middle of the nebula, like a red pupil in a monster's green eye.

The Helix Nebula was formed when a star much like our Sun died and sloughed off its skin, or outer layers. Radiation from the dead star's hot core, called a white dwarf, heats the expelled material, causing it to fluoresce with vivid colors. This cosmic beauty, termed a planetary nebula, won't last long. In about 10,000 years, its shiny clouds will fade, leaving the white dwarf and its circling comets to cool down alone in empty space.

Could this masterpiece, trillions of miles away, just now being revealed—be the work of the hands of a Grand Artist whose imagination, energy, and power have no limits?

SUPREME IMAGINATION

Exquisite Artwork from a Formerly Unknown Artist

Day after day, through their discoveries, Hubble and Spitzer relay Masterful works of cosmic art, like the Eagle Nebula, back to Earth. It is as if they have stumbled upon a Grand Gallery full of never-before-seen exquisite works of art by a formerly unknown artist.

This infrared image of the Eagle Nebula stirs emotions as it silently sings in splendor of the Grand Artist responsible for its colorful hues. This masterpiece has been acquired by a gallery 7,000 light-years away in the constellation Serpens. When you look at this scene, what you see is not just a work of cosmic art but a Grand Work of creation on a celestial scale, light-years in dimension. NASA press release, January 9, 2007:

Cosmic Epic Unfolds in Infrared: The Eagle Nebula

This majestic view taken by NASA's Spitzer Space Telescope tells an untold story of life and death in the Eagle Nebula, an industrious star-making factory located 7,000 light-years away in the Serpens constellation. The image shows the region's entire network of turbulent clouds and newborn stars in infrared light. The color green denotes cooler towers and fields of dust, including the three famous space pillars, dubbed the "Pillars of Creation," which were photographed by NASA's Hubble Space Telescope in 1995.

But it is the color red that speaks of the drama taking place in this region. Red represents hotter dust thought to have been warmed by the explosion of a massive star about 8,000 to 9,000 years ago. Since light from the Eagle Nebula takes 7,000 years to reach us, this "supernova" explosion would have appeared as an oddly bright star in our skies about 1,000 to 2,000 years ago.

According to astronomers' estimations, the explosion's blast wave would have spread outward and toppled the three pillars about 6,000 years ago (which means we wouldn't witness the destruction for another 1,000 years or so). The blast wave would have crumbled the mighty towers, exposing newborn stars that were buried inside, and triggering the birth of new ones.

Like never before, amazing data pours in day and night from Spitzer, Hubble, and other spacecraft, as if the heavens were bursting with the knowledge of unknown Superior Works of art. Could this infrared image be a self-portrait of the artist Himself sitting down to work on a masterpiece? Take a good look at this image in the lower right corner. What do you see? Does it resemble a silhouette of an artist sitting down, facing his work with an outstretched right hand, as his left hand rests on his knee with his brush in hand, as if He is explaining his technique to a young apprentice? Or is it someone with a scepter in His left hand performing an act of cosmic creation?

Whoa, that's imagination. What a brilliant work of art!

SUPREME IMAGINATION

A Young Apprentice in Training

Great artists will often take a young apprentice under their wings to teach him or her their skills. Could a peculiar pair of spiral galaxies near the constellation Canis Major reflect a Master Craftsman at work, training his young apprentice? Could this be an example as the young apprentice works to duplicate his Master's grand work of art on a galactic scale?

It seems as though the Grand Master takes special care to teach the young apprentice so that he will reflect the Supreme Imagination and Creative Genius that his Master Teacher possesses. NASA press release, November 4, 1999:

A Peculiar Pair of Spiral Galaxies

This photo image in the direction of the constellation Canis Major, shows two spiral galaxies pass by each other like majestic ships in the night. The near-collision has been caught in images taken by NASA's Hubble Space Telescope and its Wide Field Planetary Camera 2. The larger and more massive galaxy is cataloged as NGC 2207 (on the left in the Hubble Heritage image), and the smaller one on the right is IC 2163. Strong tidal forces from NGC 2207 have distorted the shape of IC 2163, flinging out stars and gas into long streamers stretching out a hundred thousand light-years toward the right-hand edge of the image.

Computer simulation calculations indicate that IC 2163 is swinging past NGC 2207 in a counterclockwise direction, having made its closest approach 40 million years ago. However, IC 2163 does not have sufficient energy to escape from the gravitational pull of NGC 2207, and is destined to be pulled back and swing past the larger galaxy again in the future. The high resolution of the Hubble telescope image reveals dust lanes in the spiral arms of NGC 2207, clearly silhouetted against IC 2163, which is in the background. Hubble also reveals a series of parallel dust filaments extending like fine brush strokes along the tidally stretched material on the right-hand side. The large concentrations of gas and dust in both galaxies may well erupt into regions of active star formation in the near future.

Trapped in their mutual orbit around each other, these two galaxies will continue to distort and disrupt each other. Eventually, billions of years from now, they will merge into a single, more massive galaxy. It is believed that many present-day galaxies, including the Milky Way, were assembled from a similar process of coalescence of smaller galaxies occurring over billions of years.

Could this pair of galaxies have been the work of a Grand Architect and his young apprentice as they worked side-by-side, creating these two Grand works of art thousands of light-years in dimension? As if performing a majestic marriage waltz, these two galaxies seem destined to unite as one. Keep in mind as you view these images, that they are living heavenly bodies in motion made up of billions of stars like our own Sun with no doubt trillions of planets that some day may support life!

Birth of Our Galaxy (Artist Concept) A Grand Architect Revealed

SUPREME IMAGINATION

The Birth of a Special Galaxy

As we look back in time at the birth of the Milky Way galaxy, through the eyes of Hubble, we are compelled to give attention to it. What we see as we look back is a construction zone on a galactic scale. As with any great architectural work, the initial stage may seem confusing and disorganized to an outsider. But to the onsite project Engineer in charge, everything is going according to plan. A spectacular work of art has been crafted.

Like someone looking at a construction zone from a distance, we do not have all the details about how this Grand Architecture was constructed. A wonderful work of supreme art is indeed our home—the Milky Way galaxy. Although we can only speculate about its beginning, it might have seemed chaotic to some observers. However, we see that order grew from that. NASA press release:

Milky Way's Birth

This is an artist's concept of the early formative years of our Milky Way galaxy, circa 12.7 billion years ago. That long ago, the majestic spiral arms of our galaxy had not yet formed; the sky was a sea of globular star clusters. The bright blue star cluster at center left is among hundreds of primeval globular star clusters that came together to build up the galaxy. This particular cluster survives today as the globular cluster M4 in Scorpius. Astronomers used Hubble to find the oldest burned-out stars–called white dwarfs–in the cluster. The dwarfs serve as "clocks" for calculating the cluster's age based on temperature. The cluster–chock full of young and blue-white stars in this artwork–probably started forming several hundred million years after the Big Bang. At right of center, the hub of the galaxy is beginning to form. Lanes of dark dust encircle a young supermassive black hole. An extragalactic jet of high-speed material beams into space from the young black hole, which is engorging itself on stars, gas and dust. A string of supernova explosions from the most massive stars in the cluster creates pink bubbles of hot gas around each star cluster.

The act of birth is miraculous when you consider that from the moment of conception a child's complete makeup is written in its DNA blueprint. Could the same be true of the birth of a galaxy? Perhaps from the moment the Milky Way was conceived in its Creator's mind, through the use of imagination, its makeup or DNA blueprint was known, and the creative work would proceed exactly as planned.

Because Hubble's orbit is inside the Milky Way galaxy, it cannot be photographed by Hubble like our neighbor, the Andromeda galaxy. But when you look at the photos of Andromeda and other galaxies, can you imagine how beautiful the Milky Way galaxy must be from an external vantage point? Does it not make you pause and respect the wonderful works of its Designer?

Milky Way Galaxy (Artist Concept)   A Grand Architect Revealed

ANDROMEDA
GALAXY

TRIANGULUM
GALAXY

THE LOCAL
GROUP

MILKY WAY
GALAXY

SUPREME IMAGINATION

Can A House Construct Itself?

It is no secret that every house was constructed by someone. Have you ever heard of a house that constructed itself? Of course not. Even a simple grass hut requires someone to build it. Does it not then seem logical that our home, the Earth, and the Milky Way galaxy it orbits within, would have been constructed by someone with an imagination? It is thought that the Milky Way was formed about the same time as the rest of the Universe—around thirteen billion years ago. When you look at the Earth and its millions of living species, including humans, you must conclude that the Grand Architect of the Universe had a very special purpose in mind when He formed the Milky Way galaxy. As far as man knows, ours is the only galaxy in the Universe to be home to living creatures. Did all of this come about for our benefit by mere chance?

As the Milky Way galaxy formed, it clustered with a local group of about three dozen other galaxies clumped in two subgroups. One formed around the Milky Way, and the other surrounded its large neighbor the Andromeda galaxy. For thousands of years, man looked up at the night sky, wondering what that white band of light across the sky was made up of. That white band came to be called the Milky Way. It took Galileo, imagination, and the invention of the telescope to discover that this white band was actually an immense group of individual stars beyond counting.

Do you suppose that it was by chance that our Sun was formed and orbits the center of the Milky Way galaxy at a distance of approximately 26,000 light-years from the galactic center? Read what Hubble observed near the center of the Galaxy. This explains why it is a good thing that we are 26,000 light-years away. NASA press release, September 16, 1999:

Hubble Spies Giant Star Clusters Near Galactic Center

Penetrating 25,000 light-years of obscuring dust and myriad stars, the Hubble telescope has provided the clearest view yet of a pair of the largest young clusters of stars inside our Milky Way Galaxy. The clusters reside less than 100 light-years from the very center of our galaxy. Having an equivalent mass greater than 10,000 stars like our Sun, the monster clusters are 10 times larger than typical young star clusters scattered throughout our Milky Way. Both clusters are destined to be ripped apart in just a few million years by gravitational tidal forces in the galaxy's core. But in the brief time they are around, they shine more brightly than any other star cluster in the galaxy.

To be in the neighborhood of such massive stars near the galactic center would make Earth uninhabitable. It would be unthinkable of a builder with an intelligent reasoning mind to build a house on the realm of a live volcano! Can there be any doubt that a Superior Intelligent Designer positioned our Sun right where it is in order for it to support intelligent life?

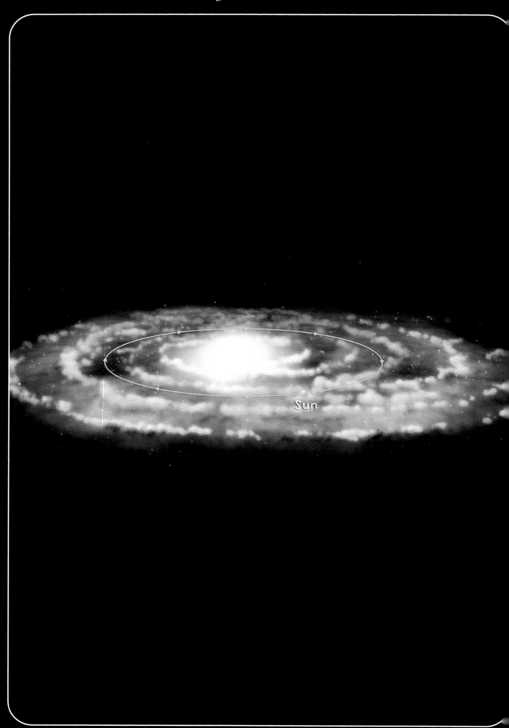

A Mother and Her Children
Perform an Orchestrated Dance

With the invention of the telescope, man began to realize that the Sun was part of a much bigger universe than what could be observed by the naked eye. Much, much later, man would know for sure that the Sun was just one of billions of suns in a galaxy that would later be named the Milky Way. Early observers saw the Sun as it rose and set each day. From their Earthly point of view, it appeared to run in a path across the heavens above.

Had they been observers outside of the galaxy, they would have known that the Earth runs in an orbit around the Sun to complete its circuit every 365 days, or one Earth year. Just like a mighty warrior, the Sun orbits the center of the Milky Way galaxy at a distance of approximately 26,000 light-years from the galactic center at the orbital velocity (i.e., speed) of about a few hundred kilometers per second, and completes its circuit in about 230 million years.

Our Sun is only one of perhaps 100 to 400 billion other suns in our galaxy, many of which are similar to the Sun, each with its own planetary systems or planets in the making. Do you not find it amazing that our moon rotates in an orbit around the Earth, as the Earth and moon together rotate and orbit around the Sun, along with the other planets and their moons? Then, in turn, the Sun rotates and orbits with all its planets and their moons, following it like young children, spinning and dancing around the Milky Way galaxy with perfect precision as if performing an orchestrated dance?

Year after year, the Sun and its children revolve with such mathematical precision and certainty that astronomers can accurately predict where they will be at any time in the future. So precise are the movements of the solar system that man was able to land on the moon some 384,403 kilometers away in 1969; and recently on May 25, 2008, NASA landed the Phoenix Mars Lander space probe on Mars to search for water and signs of life.

This orchestrated dance on a galactic scale demonstrates the superior power, knowledge, and wisdom the Designer of the Universe has, compared to that of man.

When you look at the accompanying artist's conception of the Milky Way and realize that it is one hundred thousand light-years in diameter, only then can you begin to comprehend the imagination behind our Grand Galaxy!

All the stars that the eye can distinguish in the night sky are part of the Milky Way galaxy, but aside from these relatively nearby stars, the galaxy appears as a hazy band of white light arching around the entire celestial sphere.

Do you ever look up at the night sky and gaze at all the stars in the Milky Way? Have you ever picked out a star and wondered if it has planets, and if we will one day go there to explore those new worlds? Have you ever wondered what is the purpose of all these stars?

Andromeda Galaxy M31

SUPREME IMAGINATION

Can You Name All The Stars?

The ancient text that invites us to *"Look up into the heavens."* and asks *"Who created all the stars?"* also states He is *"calling each by its name."* Imagine, not only does the Grand Architect of the Universe know the exact number of all the stars, but he calls each one by name. What human could come close to accurately counting all the stars, let along naming them?

The Milky Way is a "barred spiral galaxy." It consists of a bar-shaped core region surrounded by a disk of gas, dust, and stars. Within the disk region are several arm structures that spiral outward in a logarithmic spiral shape. Its galactic center harbors a compact object of very large mass, strongly suspected to be a super-massive black hole. It contains our solar system—the Sun, the Earth, and other planets, as well as star clusters, asteroids, nebula, and assorted cosmic phenomenon. The Milky Way is a relatively small galaxy among billions of other galaxies within the universe. It is thought to contain 100 to 400 billion or more stars, yes that is 100,000,000,000 to 400,000,000,000! Some galaxies are thought to contain a trillion or more stars. The Milky Way belongs to a local group of galaxies, comprising over thirty other galaxies, including the Great Andromeda Galaxy M31.

The diameter of our galaxy is so vast that if you could travel as fast as the speed of light (186,282 miles *a second*) it would take you 100,000 years to cross it! How many miles would you have to travel? Well, since light travels about six trillion (6,000,000,000,000) miles in a year, multiply that by 100,000 and you have the answer—Our Milky Way galaxy is about 600 quadrillion (600,000,000,000,000,000) miles in diameter.

Since the Hubble and other space telescopes are in orbit inside the Milky Way, it is not possible to photograph it like other neighboring galaxies. For this reason, it has ably photographed the sister galaxies, such as the Great Andromeda Galaxy. It is thought by some that if we could see our galaxy from a distance, it would look much like the Andromeda Galaxy.

Consider the Andromeda Galaxy's size. It is a spiral galaxy approximately two-and-a-half million light-years away in the constellation Andromeda and is thought to be 220,000 light-years in diameter, containing one trillion stars. Yes, that is 1,000,000,000,000 stars.

Are you not awestruck by the sheer number of stars in these two galaxies alone? It is incomprehensible for man to even consider naming all the stars in two galaxies, let alone in the entire universe. Is it not logical that the One who made them would be able to name each one by its own unique name? Is not His naming the stars proof that His Imagination has no limits?

As you view this image of the Majestic Andromeda Galaxy, pause for a moment and ponder what imagination and source of power is responsible for this Grand Symphony of stars, then review the inspiring words Isaiah wrote.

Details About the Birth of a Planet

In the beginning God created the heavens and the earth.[2] The earth was formless and empty, and darkness covered the deep waters ...[3] Then God said, "Let there be light." And there was light. —Genesis 1:1-3

These words, recorded millennia ago, may prove to be the most profound words ever recorded. This simple statement left out the details of how the Universe and the Earth formed. It is becoming clear that we are now getting the details of this spectacular event. Hubble has revealed the Universe began to form 13.7 billion years ago and the Earth 4.54 billion years ago. It appears that Hubble and Spitzer may have uncovered the truth about this long-debated creation account.

It is now known that the Universe formed first, and then the Earth in the same sequence as stated in Genesis. However, something more specific and revealing has come to light from the discoveries of these two telescopes. You will learn on the following pages how they have captured a scientific footprint of planet formation that appears to confirm the Genesis account of creation to be scientifically accurate. They have, in recent years, discovered that the ingredients for life find their way into the dense dust clouds that swirl around new-forming stars.

It is in these dense dark dust lanes that a moist slurry of dirt and rock debris begin to clump together to form rocky planets like our Earth. In the case of Earth this process lasted for billions of years as the planet was taking shape as it matured. During this process the planet at some phase could be described as being in a formless and dark state as it was shrouded in dust hidden from the light of the Sun. (See images on pages 82-88.) This planet-forming phase appears to correspond with the statement made at Genesis1:2. *The earth was formless and empty, and darkness covered the deep waters.*

As the planet matures, the dust and debris is sucked up by the planet like a giant vacuum cleaner. During its later stage the planet is slowly exposed to the Sun's light. Leftover material is eventually blown out by solar wind or pushed out by gravitational interactions with the planets as Hubble and Spitzer discovered with a Sun-like star called HD 107146. (See image on page 90.) During this process the planet could be described as having light appear, after a long period of darkness inside the cloud of dust. This planet-forming phase appears to correspond with day one at Genesis 1:3. *"Let there be light." And there was light.* If Galileo were alive today, he would no doubt agree that the discoveries revealed by Hubble and Spitzer appear to provide conclusive scientific evidence that the Genesis writer recorded an accurate overview of creation. While he had a conflict with the religion of his day, Galileo had no conflict with the Bible and its creation account. He realized the writers of the Scriptures wrote in a simple style, from the perspective of the terrestrial world and not from the heavens above. (See NASA video at http://www.spitzer.caltech.edu/video-audio/691-ssc2004-08v3-Forming-a-Planetary-Gap)

ACT V

A GRAND ARCHITECT
REVEALED AND COMPLETED

A SPECIAL STAR IS BORN

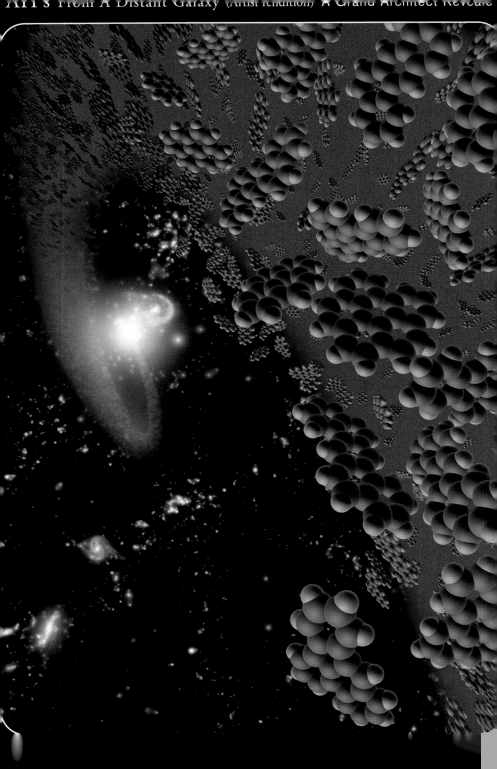

The Miracle of Life

The question of where life started has been pondered for millennia. Even today, evident by our unending search for the origins of life, man is still, in essence, saying, "I want the details." Little by little, the details are being revealed as a result of man's imagination through the use of space technology. NASA press release, July 28, 2005:

Spitzer Finds Life Components in Young Universe

NASA's Spitzer Space Telescope has found the ingredients for life all the way back to a time when the universe was a mere youngster. Using Spitzer, scientists have detected organic molecules in galaxies when our universe was one-fourth of its current age of about 14 billion years. This artist's conception symbolically represents complex organic molecules, known as polycyclic aromatic hydrocarbons, seen in the early universe. These large molecules, known as polycyclic aromatic hydrocarbons, are comprised of carbon and hydrogen. The molecules are considered to be among the building blocks of life.

These complex molecules are very common on Earth. They form any time carbon-based materials are not burned completely. They can be found in sooty exhaust from cars and airplanes, and in charcoal broiled hamburgers and burnt toast. The molecules, pervasive in galaxies like our own Milky Way, play a significant role in star and planet formation. Spitzer is the first telescope to see polycyclic aromatic hydrocarbons so early—10 billion years further back in time than seen previously.

Organic molecules are the chemicals of life, compounds composed of more than one type of element that are found in and produced by living organisms. The four major classes of organic molecules include carbohydrates, proteins, lipids, and nucleic acids.

What imagination on the part of the Grand Architect. Billions of years ago, He used the basic building blocks for life to form our planet. They would later be used by Him to create a variety of life forms, including humans, from the dust of the ground. We may never have a complete understanding of the creative process used by this Grand Architect; but rest assured, our understanding will continue to grow with each generation, especially as we build upon our knowledge and use our own imaginations to explore the world around us.

On the following pages you will get a pictorial overview from the Hubble and Spitzer telescopes of just how planets form. This information will give you a better understanding of how our Earth was transformed in the dark, from formless cosmic dust and rock into a beautiful planet full of life, sustained by the light of our Sun. It appears we now have hard physical evidence pouring in from space that validates the Genesis account of creation to be scientifically accurate.

How could someone millennia ago record the fundamental basics of creation and accurately describe what is being discovered through sophisticated space technology today, unless someone who knew the details told them?

SUPREME IMAGINATION

Simply Dust in the Quasar Wind

According to NASA, the hit song that proclaimed "All we are is dust in the wind" may have some cosmic truth to it. New findings from NASA's Spitzer Space Telescope suggest that space dust, the same stuff that makes up living creatures and planets, was manufactured in large quantities in the winds of black holes that populated our early universe. NASA press release, October 9, 2007:

Dust in the Quasar Wind

Dusty grains—including tiny specks of the minerals found in the gemstones peridot, sapphires, and rubies—can be seen blowing in the winds of a quasar, or active black hole, in this artist's concept. The quasar is at the center of a distant galaxy. Astronomers using NASA's Spitzer Space Telescope found evidence that such quasar winds might have forged these dusty particles in the very early universe. The findings are another clue in an ongoing cosmic mystery: where did all the dust in our young universe come from? Dust is crucial for efficient star formation as it allows the giant clouds where stars are born to cool quickly and collapse into new stars. Once a star has formed, dust is also needed to make planets and living creatures.

Dust has been seen as far back as when the universe was less than a tenth of its current age, but how did it get there? Most dust in our current epoch forms in the winds of evolved stars that did not exist when the universe was young. Theorists had predicted that winds from quasars growing in the centers of distant galaxies might be a source of this dust. While the environment close to a quasar is too hot for large molecules like dust grains to survive, dust has been found in the cooler, outer regions. Astronomers now have evidence that dust is created in these outer winds. Using Spitzer's infrared spectrograph instrument, scientists found a wealth of dust grains in a quasar called PG2112+059 located at the center of a galaxy 8 billion light-years away.

It appears that some of this cosmic dust was mixed with water and sculpted into a living work of art that has been placed in a gallery known as the Milky Way—the work of art called planet Earth. From that masterpiece, the Sculptor then formed human life out of the basic life-building elements of dust from the ground we now walk upon. Do you not find it most amazing that everything we have, through one form or another, like ourselves, was formed from this cosmic dust? The chair you are sitting on right now, this book, your house and every item in it, your food, your clothes, your car—everything is nothing more than some of this wonderful cosmic dust that was once blowing in the wind of the early universe. Imagine that!

As we unravel the wonderful truths about our past, it only strengthens our resolve to dig ever deeper for a clearer understanding of the Superior wisdom that went into the design of the cosmic earthly clay we are made of. What we are learning as we probe this incredible universe is that our insatiable quest is worth the effort and sacrifice.

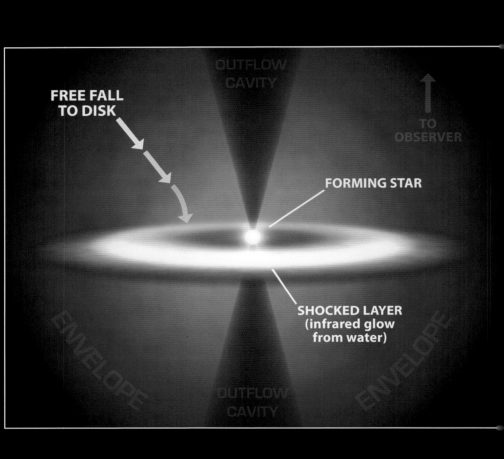

Water—The Liquid Miracle

In order for Earth to sustain future life, it will need vast quantities of water upon it. Observe how water may have been placed upon the Earth's surface like the star and planetary birth scene now being played out in the star system called NGC 1333-IRAS 4B. NASA press release, August 29, 2007:

Water Vapor Seen "Raining Down" on Young Star System

NASA's Spitzer Space Telescope has detected enough water vapor to fill the oceans on Earth five times inside the collapsing nest of a forming star system. Astronomers say the water vapor is pouring down from the system's natal cloud and smacking into a dusty disk where planets are thought to form. The observations provide the first direct look at how water, an essential ingredient for life as we know it, begins to make its way into planets, possibly even rocky ones like our own.

For the first time, we are seeing water being delivered to the region where planets will most likely form. The star system, called NGC 1333-IRAS 4B, is still growing inside a cool cocoon of gas and dust. Within this cocoon, circling around the embryonic star is a burgeoning, warm disk of planet-forming materials. The new Spitzer data indicate that ice from the stellar embryo's outer cocoon is falling toward the forming star and vaporizing as it hits the disk. "On Earth, water arrived in the form of icy asteroids and comets. Water also exists mostly as ice in the dense clouds that form stars." This diagram illustrates the earliest journeys of water in a young, forming star system. Stars are born out of icy cocoons of gas and dust. NGC 1333-IRAS 4B is located in a pretty star-forming region approximately 1,000 light-years away in the constellation Perseus.

Can you picture a scene where, billions of years ago, the warm moist disk of materials orbiting our Sun began to clump and collect together under the forces of gravity? This led to the birth of our planet. Can you imagine how it began to grow, as a young child would under its parents' watchful care? Once it was fully mature, it was then swaddled in a blanket of water and thick gloom of clouds? The star- and planet-forming events now unfolding trillions of miles away, seen through the eyes of Spitzer, appear to shed new light on how this liquid miracle may have arrived on Earth.

Water covers 70.9% of the Earth's surface, and is vital for all known forms of life. On Earth, it is found mostly in oceans and other large water bodies, with 1.6% of water below ground in aquifers and 0.001% in the air as vapor, clouds, and precipitation.

The very existence of life itself on Earth is based on it. In fact, water is the main ingredient of most living things. The human body has been described as a "virtual walking sack of precariously contained fluids." About two-thirds of your total weight is water, with water comprising as much as three-fourths of your brain and muscles. What a wonderful substance!

SUPREME IMAGINATION

A Special Star is Born

From cosmic dust swirling for billions of years, to a brilliant shining star, the star at the center of our solar system came to life. This star amongst trillions would prove to be a special star to eventually give birth to a very special planet, our home, the Earth. If we could look back in time to see the birth of our Sun from a cloud of gases and cosmic dust, perhaps the scene we would see would be much like the one that Spitzer witnessed 600 light-years away in the constellation Cygnus in the Star system L1014, depicted in this artist's conception. NASA press release, November 9, 2004:

Spitzer Sees Ice and Warm Glows in Dark and Dusty Places

In this artist's conception, we peer through the dark dust of L1014 to witness the birth of a star. NASA's Spitzer Space Telescope has detected a faint, warm object inside the apparently starless core of a small, dense molecular cloud. If, as astronomers suspect, there is a young star deep inside the dusty core, it would have a structure similar to this illustration. Dark dust from the cloud, attracted by the gravity of the newborn star, forms a disc as it spirals inward. Often, the hidden birth of a star is heralded by bipolar outflows, jets of material moving outward from the star's poles. Although astronomers do see a faint "fan-shaped nebulosity" where they might expect the jet to be, the existence of the jet has yet to be confirmed.

Two new results from NASA's Spitzer Space Telescope released today are helping astronomers better understand how stars form out of thick clouds of gas and dust, and how the molecules in those clouds ultimately become planets. Using Spitzer's infrared eyes, a team of astronomers of the University of Texas at Austin probed dozens of these dusty cores to gain insight into conditions that are needed for stars to form.

In one discovery, Spitzer's infrared eyes have peered into the place where planets are born—the center of a dusty disc surrounding an infant star— and spied the icy ingredients of planets and comets. This is the first definitive detection of ices in planet-forming discs. This disc resembles closely how we imagine our own solar system looked when it was only a few hundred thousand years old. It has the right size, and the central star is small and probably stable enough to support a water-rich planetary system for billions of years into the future.

Who could imagine that from a cloud of cosmic dust, such a beautiful life-sustaining work of Art could be sculpted? Just like a sculptor with his clay, the Grand Sculptor of the Universe used just the right combination of life-sustaining materials to express His imagination on a grand scale for our benefit, when from cosmic dust He formed our Sun that gives life to this planet we call home.

The images from page 80 to 90 represent the formation of our Sun and solar system, including planet Earth and its moon as they were born in dense darkness, to finally emerge into the light in its more mature phase. This entire period is a period thought to be billions of years long.

SUPREME IMAGINATION

Star Dust Collects to Form Planets

Galileo may have wondered how the Earth was formed and what held it in place. He did not have the benefit of an infrared space telescope to give him any clues. Like a curious child, he sought answers to those questions. Only now are some of these long-hidden secrets being revealed as man looks back in time, aided by the technology of Hubble and Spitzer.

These artist concepts of the Spitzer and Hubble space telescope's discoveries of planets forming from the cosmic dust debris of newly forming stars can give us some clues. Hubble and Spitzer are uncovering secrets as to how our Sun and solar system—including Earth—were formed. Notice the progressive stages. This is how the star forms first, creating a disk of cosmic dust and debris. The planets were then formed from the dust lanes in darkness. All the dust and debris blocked the Sun's light until the dust and debris eventually dissipated, finally allowing the parent Sun to provide unrestricted life-sustaining light. NASA press release, August 29, 2007:

Star System Called NGC 1333-IRAS 4B

In the new Spitzer study, water also serves as an important tool for studying long-sought details of the planet formation process. By analyzing what's happening to the water in NGC 1333-IRAS 4B, the astronomers are learning about its disk. For example, they calculated the disk's density (at least 10 billion hydrogen molecules per cubic centimeter or 160 billion hydrogen molecules per cubic inch); its dimensions (a radius bigger than the average distance between Earth and Pluto); and its temperature (170 Kelvin, or minus 154 degrees Fahrenheit).

Water is easier to detect than other molecules, so we can use it as a probe to look at more brand-new disks and study their physics and chemistry, this will teach us a lot about how planets form. We have captured a unique phase of a young star's evolution, when the stuff of life is moving dynamically into an environment where planets could form. NGC 1333-IRAS 4B's central stellar embryo is still "feeding" off the material collapsing around it and growing in size. At this early stage, astronomers cannot tell how large the star will ultimately become.

As new information pours in from space we are getting a much clearer blueprint of how our Sun and Earth formed. The great mystery of just how Earth was created from cosmic dust is beginning to unravel before our very eyes. (http://www.spitzer. caltech.edu/video-audio/689-ssc2004-08v2-Icy-Organics-in-Planet-Forming-Discs)

According to a new study by Australian astronomers, there are "70 sextillion stars in the known universe." Assuming that many, if not all stars, may eventually develop planets during their life cycle, it is reasonable to assume that if each star developed just six planets there could be 420 sextillion planets in the universe (420,000,000,000,000,000,000,000). That astronomical number significantly increases the likelihood of a large number of inhabitable planets in the universe!

A Dusty Construction Zone

As the cosmic dust masses were brought together billions of years ago to form our solar system, perhaps Earth's dusty construction zone looked similar to this scene discovered by Spitzer in the Ophiuchus constellation. NASA press release, December 20, 2005:

Partial Ingredients for DNA and Protein Found Around Star

NASA's Spitzer Space Telescope has discovered some of life's most basic ingredients in the dust swirling around a young star. The ingredients—gaseous precursors to DNA and protein—were detected in the star's terrestrial planet zone, a region where rocky planets such as Earth are thought to be born. The findings represent the first time that these gases, called acetylene and hydrogen cyanide, have been found in a terrestrial planet zone outside of our own.

This infant system might look a lot like ours did billions of years ago, before life arose on Earth, said scientists of Leiden Observatory in the Netherlands and the Dutch space research institute called SRON.

Scientists spotted the organic, or carbon-containing, gases around a star called IRS 46. The star is in the Ophiuchus (pronounced OFF-ee-YOO-kuss), or "snake carrier," constellation about 375 light-years from Earth. This constellation harbors a huge cloud of gas and dust in the process of a major stellar baby boom. Like most of the young stars here and elsewhere, IRS 46 is circled by a flat disk of spinning gas and dust that might ultimately clump together to form planets. When the astronomers probed this star's disk with Spitzer's powerful infrared spectrometer instrument, they were surprised to find the molecular "barcodes" of large amounts of acetylene and hydrogen cyanide gases, as well as carbon dioxide gas. The team observed 100 similar young stars, but only one, IRS 46, showed unambiguous signs of the organic mix.

Here on Earth, the molecules are believed to have arrived billions of years ago, possibly via comets or comet dust that rained down from the sky. Acetylene and hydrogen cyanide link up together in the presence of water to form some of the chemical units of life's most essential compounds, DNA and protein. These chemical units are several of the 20 amino acids that make up protein and one of the four chemical bases that make up DNA. Follow-up observations with the W. M. Keck Telescope atop Mauna Kea in Hawaii confirmed the Spitzer findings and suggested the presence of a wind emerging from the inner region of IRS 46's disk. This wind will blow away debris in the disk, clearing the way for the possible formation of Earth-like planets.

Is it not amazing that each of us, this Earth, and everything around us were created from the cosmic dust lanes of a **protoplanetary disk**? From this clay we were sculpted into living works of art by a Grand Sculptor. Without this life-giving process all we would be is simply a lump of clay. At this early stage of formation the Earth would have been formless lumps of dirt and rock clumping together.

Planet Danger Zone

While imagination is the driving force behind all things new, great wisdom also was evidently used in constructing our Sun in just the right location in the galaxy. Consider a new study from NASA's Spitzer Space Telescope. NASA press release, April 18, 2007:

Highway to the Danger Zone

"The further on the edge, the hotter the intensity," sings Kenny Loggins in **Danger Zone,** *a song made famous by the movie* **Top Gun.** *The same words ring true for young, cooler stars like our Sun that live in the danger zones around scorching hot stars, called O-stars. The closer a young, maverick star happens to be to a super hot O-star, the more likely its burgeoning planets will be blasted into space.*

This artist's concept illustrates the process in action. An O-star can be seen near the top right, just behind a young, cooler star and its swirling disk of planet-forming material. Disks like this one, called protoplanetary disks, are where planets are born. Gas and dust in a disk clump together into tiny balls that sweep through the material, growing in size to eventually become full-grown planets. The young star happens to lie within the "danger zone" around the O-star, which means that it is too close to the hot star to keep its disk. Radiation and winds from the O-star are boiling and blowing away the material, respectively. This process, called photoevaporation, takes anywhere from 100,000 to about 1,000,000 years. Without a disk, the young star will not be able to produce planets.

Our own sun and its suite of planets might have grown up on the edge of an O-star's danger zone before migrating to its current, spacious home. However, we know that our young sun didn't linger for too long in any hazardous territory, or our planets, and life, wouldn't be here today. NASA's Spitzer Space Telescope surveyed the danger zones around five O-stars in the Rosette nebula. It was able to determine that the zones are spheres with a radius of approximately 1.6 light-years, or 10 trillion miles. (http://www.spitzer.caltech.edu/video-audio/950-ssc2007-08v2-Highway-to-the-Danger-Zone-)

Great wisdom is evident in this Grand Design when we consider the fine balance needed to sustain life that is found in the design of the Earth. There are so many factors that would have made life on Earth impossible if the conditions were not just perfect. Our solar system is like a finely tuned engine that runs so smooth we don't even realize it is even in motion.

As you look at this image to the left it is easy to imagine what Hubble and Spitzer have discovered inside massive rotating clouds of star dust like this one. Inside this cocoon of dust is where planets like Earth are born in total darkness. In its early stage the planet is a formless slurry of rock and dirt, but slowly this material smashes and clumps together to become a rotating clumpy ball that eventually grows into a planet as its rotation and the forces of gravity grow.

SUPREME IMAGINATION

Planets Born in Darkness

No one really knows exactly when the Earth was formed or how long it must have taken to bring to completion. The most recent consensus from scientists suggests the Earth is approximately four-and-a-half billion years old. All great works of art require considerable amounts of time, care, and craftsmanship, and the larger the work, the greater the time required.

Imagine if you can, looking back in time. You are peering into the Universe through a giant window, scrutinizing our solar system and observing the formation of our Sun and its planets. What you witness would no doubt take your breath away. You would be in awe of the magnitude and precision of it all as each planet spun in its own orbit around the Sun, each one taking on its own personality like a newborn child, sucking up cosmic dust as it grew from an infant to a full-grown planet.

Perhaps the planet-forming scene you witness would be like the scene that is now being witnessed 450 light-years away in a solar system called UX Tau A. This stellar prodigy has been spotted by NASA's Spitzer Space Telescope. NASA press release, November 28, 2007:

Youthful Star Sprouts Planets Early

Astronomers suspect this system's central Sun-like star, which is just one million years old, may already be surrounded by young planets. Scientists hope the finding will provide insight into when planets began to form in our own solar system. Such dusty disks are where planets are thought to be born. Dust grains clump together like snowballs to form larger rocks, and then the bigger rocks collide to form the cores of planets. When rocks revolve around their central star, they act like cosmic vacuum cleaners, picking up all the gas and dust in their path and creating gaps. Spitzer saw a gap in UX Tau A's disc, which in our solar system, this gap would occupy the space between Mercury and Pluto.

During the earliest phase of planet formation the earth would have been a mass of moist dirt and rock clumping together as it grew in size over time, much like a snowball as it rolls in the snow. This process took place inside a dense cloud of dust as it revolved around the Sun, as seen in the images on the previous pages.

This planet-forming phase observed by Spitzer, reveals how planets are formed in darkness in their younger stage. The Sun's light would have been blocked from Earth for perhaps billions of years, much like what we see in these images. As the dense dark dust lanes between the Earth and the Sun are sucked up by the Earth, Venus, and Mercury like giant vacuum cleaners, the older, more mature Earth would gradually over time, emerge from darkness into the light.

These dusty dark phases Spitzer has witnessed appear to correspond scientifically to the period prior to day one of the Genesis account. The earth at some stage was formless and shrouded in darkness. This gives a great deal of credibility to the Genesis account. *The earth was formless and empty, and darkness covered the deep waters.* – Genesis 1:2

Let There Be Light

This scene of a Sun-like star called HD 107146, located eighty-eight light-years away, observed by Hubble and Spitzer, provides insight on how light first reached Earth. After billions of years in darkness, it appears the remaining dust and debris blocking the Sun's light would have been polished away making day and night distinguishable on Earth. NASA press release, December 9, 2004:

Spitzer and Hubble Capture Evolving Planetary Systems

Two of NASA's Great Observatories, the Spitzer Space Telescope and the Hubble Space Telescope, have provided astronomers an unprecedented look at dusty planetary debris around stars the size of our Sun. Spitzer has discovered for the first time dusty discs around mature, Sun-like stars known to have planets. Hubble captured the most detailed image ever of a brighter disc circling a much younger Sun-like star. The findings offer snapshots of the process by which our own solar system evolved, from its dusty and chaotic beginnings to its more settled present-day state. Young stars have huge reservoirs of planet-building materials, while older ones have only left-over piles of rubble. Hubble saw the reservoirs and Spitzer, the rubble. This demonstrates how the two telescopes complement each other. The young star observed by Hubble is 50 million to 250 million years old. This is old enough to theoretically have gas planets, but young enough that rocky planets like Earth may still be forming. The six older stars studied by Spitzer average 4 billion years old, nearly the same age as the Sun. They are known to have gas planets, and rocky planets may also be present. Prior to these findings, rings of planetary debris, or "debris discs," around stars the size of the Sun had rarely been observed, because they are fainter and more difficult to see than those around more massive stars. The new Hubble image gives us the best look so far at reflected light from a disc around a star the mass of the Sun, it shows one of the possible pasts of our own solar system. Debris discs around older stars the same size and age as our Sun, including those hosting known planets, are even harder to detect. These discs are 10 to 100 times thinner than the ones around young stars. Spitzer's highly sensitive infrared detectors were able to sense their warm glow for the first time. Rocky planets arise out of large clouds of dust that envelop young stars. Dust particles collide and stick together until a planet eventually forms. Sometimes the accumulating bodies crash together and shatter. Debris from these collisions collects into giant doughnut-shaped discs, the centers of which may be carved out by orbiting planets. With time, the discs fade and a smaller, stable debris disc, like the comet-filled Kuiper Belt in our own solar system, is all that is left.

During this later phase, the Earth gradually emerged from darkness! These findings by Hubble and Spitzer show that as the planet matured the dense dark dust was polished away allowing the Sun's diffused light to filter through, making day and night distinguishable upon the surface as the Earth rotated on its axis. This light-revealing phase appears to correspond scientifically to day one of the Genesis account. *Let there be light, and there was light.*–Genesis 1:3   91

SUPREME IMAGINATION

Life-Giving Light Emerges

As seen on pages 80 to 89, Spitzer, in epic fashion, has captured a footprint of how Earth-like planets are formed from clouds of dust and debris in dense darkness that correspond to Genesis, prior to day one. Also seen on pages 90 and 91, Spitzer, along with Hubble, has revealed that planets are gradually exposed to sunlight as they mature and the dust cloud is polished away making night and day distinguishable, corresponding to Genesis during day one. These phases planets undergo in the process of forming appear to correspond to Genesis 1:2, 3 and provide a blueprint of proof to the scientific accuracy of the Genesis record. This scientific evidence adds a great deal of creditability to the creation account of Genesis. (See Video) http://www.youtube.com/watch?v=1KMd-5MVF_E)

As the Earth cooled, some of the water separated from Earth's surface in the form of a dense cloud mass. This created an expanse between it and the water left on the Earth. As the remaining water on the Earth pressed down on its surface, dry land slowly appeared as oceans formed.

In order to prepare Earth for living creatures, including humans, an oxygen-filled atmosphere was needed. This has been provided through the ingenious engineering process called photosynthesis. The Sun's diffused light reaching the Earth changed everything. It set into motion an orderly process that prepared the Earth in stages to eventually support intelligent human life. Green vegetation began to blanket the earth as a food source for sea life, flying creatures, land animals, and finally—humans.

The existence of life on Earth is fueled by light from the Sun. Most autotrophs, such as plants, use the energy of sunlight, combined with carbon dioxide and water, to produce simple sugars—a process known as photosynthesis. These sugars are then used as building blocks and in other synthetic pathways which allow the organism to grow. Nearly all life either depends on this process directly as a source of energy, or indirectly as the ultimate source of the energy in their food.

Just as a farmer prepares his fields in order to successfully grow his crops it appears the Grand Architect of Earth took great care to prepare the Earth for life to flourish in abundance.

The images from page 90 to 102 represent the final progressive and orderly phases the Earth underwent for its completion in order to prepare it for the arrival of intelligent human life. It is not clear how long these periods would have been, evidence reveals that a considerable amount of time passed before humans arrived on the scene.

Interestingly these episodes give validity to the six creative days or periods of the Genesis account. Hubble and Spitzer have revealed as Galileo expressed, "not all scripture can be taken literally." Often, throughout the Scriptures a day is referred to an unspecified amount of time and not a literal twenty-four hour day. That line of thought appears to correspond to the recent scientific discoveries made by these two telescopes.

SUPREME IMAGINATION

The Heart of a Planet

Earth was eventually covered with a blanket of green vegetation of every kind. As the heartbeat of the planet it provides nourishment for a vast array of living creatures, including humans.

Earth's soil is much more than lifeless dirt. Just scoop up a handful of it and you will find a complex medium for growth, bursting with organisms. Just two pounds may contain well over 500 billion bacteria, one billion funguses, and up to 500 million multi-cellular creatures, from insects to worms. Many of these organisms work together, breaking down organic matter—such as leaf litter and animal waste—while extracting nitrogen, which they convert into forms that plants can absorb. They also change the carbon into carbon dioxide and other compounds.

Vegetation, from grasses to trees, is the foundation of the "food chain" on the land. This is because no animal can manufacture its own food. But plants do this work by the complex process of photosynthesis, a process not yet fully understood or duplicated by man. Scientists who study plant species are called botanists. Botanists have, thus far, identified more than 300,000 species of plants on our amazing planet.

Not only does vegetation provide needed oxygen, it supplies our every desire for food and scenic beauty. See Earth truly come alive as its heart beats in a way you have never imagined. You will be amazed when you view the planet animation imaging by NASA's "SeaWiFS Biosphere Animation" at: http://oceancolor.gsfc.nasa.gov/SeaWiFS/HTML/SeaWiFS.BiosphereAnimation.70W.html

See for yourself how the heart of the Earth appears to be beating as the seasons come and go. The Earth's vegetation expands over the planet each growing season, and then retracts in this animated display, as if the Earth's heart were pulsating and providing life to all! The earth appears to be alive!

Look at the endless variety of plant life on the Earth. It, too, came from the dust of the ground. This phenomenon emanated from an Imagination far superior to that of man. As caretakers of the Earth, it is man's responsibility to make sure that an environmental balance is maintained. However, we are doing a poor job of stewardship of the planet, considering the multitude of serious environmental issues facing man today.

Sometime during or after vegetation began to blanket the Earth, but prior to living creatures, luminaries like the sun, moon and stars, gradually became visible from the surface of the Earth. This may have occurred due to the remaining dust disc in the solar system fading as it was blown away by solar winds, leaving only the Kuipler Belt. With the atmosphere clear, and luminaries clearly visible in the day and night sky it would make it possible for later sea life, flying creatures, land animals, and humans to easily navigate the Earth. Prior to this period they would have had difficulty navigating without these points of light to navigate by.

This progressive, orderly development of Earth shows the imagination and wisdom that went into the design of the universe. This phase appears to correspond with day four of the Genesis account.

Exotic Creatures Fill the Sea

After the oceans developed an abundance of plankton and algae that served as food, an endless variety of sea life began to fill the sea.

Can you recall your very first encounter with sea creatures? It may have been a goldfish in a fishbowl or a sea horse glimpsed on your first trip to an aquarium, or a shark! Can you remember your first reaction? Was it one of excitement and curiosity?

Perhaps you were at the beach and you saw dolphins playing and jumping out of the water near shore. Did you have a desire to go out and join in their play?

The oceans are home to some of the most amazing creatures on our planet. Children and adults alike are fascinated by the animals that call the ocean their home, especially whales, sharks, manatees, seals, dolphins, and sea turtles.

Marine life is a vast resource of hundreds of thousands of species, which not only provide food, medicine, and raw materials, but also help to support recreation and tourism all over the world. At a fundamental level, marine life helps determine the very nature of our planet. Marine organisms contribute significantly to the oxygen cycle, and are involved in the regulation of the Earth's climate. Shorelines are in part shaped and protected by marine life, and some marine organisms even help create new land.

A large amount of all life on Earth exists in the oceans. Exactly what percentage is unknown, since many ocean species have yet to be discovered. While the oceans comprise about 71% of the Earth's surface, due to their depth, they encompass about 300 times the habitable volume of the terrestrial habitats on Earth.

Microscopic life undersea is incredibly diverse and still poorly understood. For example, the role of viruses in marine ecosystems is just now beginning to be explored, well into the twenty-first century.

Plant life under the ocean is widespread and very diverse. Microscopic photosynthetic algae contribute a larger proportion of the world's photosynthetic output than all the terrestrial forests combined.

Reefs comprise some of the densest and most diverse habitats in the world. The best-known reefs are tropical coral reefs, which exist in most tropical waters. However, reefs can also exist in cold water. Reefs are built up by corals and other calcium-depositing animals, usually on top of a rocky outcrop on the ocean floor.

If you have ever gone snorkeling or diving over a coral reef, you may have been amazed at the kaleidoscope of colorful fish and sea creatures in all sorts of shapes and sizes. The next time you find yourself underwater, ask yourself: *Am I here for their enjoyment and pleasure or are they here for mine?* Once again, we see evidence of a Grand Designer with Superior imagination even in the deepest depths of the sea.

Learning From the Experts

As you gaze up at the sky, you notice an eagle high above with its wings spread wide as it glides effortlessly along the wind current; you dream of flying just like that. You think of how you could traverse the landscape from high above to get a better perspective of the countryside. You think of the exhilaration you would experience as you dive from high above, then glide down across the treetops before soaring up once again to breathtaking heights.

Perhaps your thoughts are not much different from those of Orville and Wilber Wright as their observations of birds' aerodynamics braided with their imagination to discover the mechanics of the first airplane. Due to man's superior mind and imagination, birds are no match for man's modern-day flying machines, yet aeronautical engineers still study them to learn more secrets from their physiology and natural flying abilities.

If it were not for these intriguing creatures, the Hubble telescope most likely would not exist and you would not be witnessing the Grand Drama it is now recording. There is thought to be about 10,000 living species of birds, and over one million insects of every shape and form. Some are so strange and unique we have yet to discover their purpose. From his beginning, man has been the student of countless creatures that inhabit this Earth with us. They teach us how to do some of the things they do naturally, like flying!

When we look closely, it is amazing what we are learning from even very small creatures. Take, for example, the monarch butterfly which has a brain about the size of the tip of a ballpoint pen. Yet the monarch butterfly migrates as far as 1,800 miles from Canada to a small patch of forest in Mexico. How does it find its way?

We have discovered that monarch butterflies have a solar compass that is fixed to the position of the Sun. These insects also use a remarkably accurate circadian clock—a biological function based on the twenty-four-hour day—to make corrections for the Sun's movement. As scientists study these tiny creatures' inner timepiece, they hope to gain further insight into the circadian clocks of humans and animals. This may help us to better understand time and space.

The fastest of all flying animals is the peregrine falcon, which has been recorded flying at speeds in excess of 200 miles per hour when diving. Most flying animals need to travel forward at a minimum speed to stay aloft. However, some creatures can stay in the same spot, known as hovering, either by rapidly flapping the wings, as do hummingbirds, hoverflies, and dragonflies. The bar-headed goose, *Anser indicus,* is one of the world's highest flying birds, having been seen at an altitude of 33,382 feet.

When you look at the beautifully colored macaw to the left, do you reason that it got its colors through chance or do you recognize that it was designed that way for its survival and for our pleasure to look at? When you consider the complex navigational system of the monarch butterfly, is it logical to believe it is the product of chance? Or is it one more piece of evidence pointing to the inevitable existence of an intelligent Designer?

Man's Beloved Friends and Teachers

Can you member your first encounter with a land animal? Perhaps it was a puppy or kitten. Can you remember how much joy it brought you when you would play with it, or cuddle it in your arms, or when it licked you on the face? When you look at the panda to the left does it not make you want to just pet it or scratch it behind its ears and play with it? It's a natural human emotion to be drawn to animals.

It is clear that animal life on this planet was put here for the benefit and enjoyment of man. From the very beginning, we have observed and studied animals and thus gained a vast wealth of knowledge from them. We have copied their actions and behavior to develop new products like airplanes, submarines, and countless other inventions.

Though humans have shared the planet with millions of other creatures for thousands of years, we know surprisingly little about our neighbors—we do not even know exactly how many animals call Earth home. There are over 1.7 million identified species of animals and many millions yet to be named. We have only scratched the surface of understanding animal life. Some scientists contend we have discovered a mere ten percent of all living things on this planet.

Did you know the cheetah is recognized as the fastest land animal in the world; it reaches speeds upwards of seventy miles per hour, and Pronghorn antelopes can reach speeds of up to sixty miles per hour. Are you aware that a polar bear can jump over a twenty-foot crack in the ice, and can swim very long distances in near-freezing water because it has a thick layer of blubber to keep it warm?

Animals are designed in such a way that they have a general fear of man as their superior. Wild animals normally prefer to retreat from man's presence, however they do attack when provoked, wounded, cornered, or surprised. Some animals sometimes become man-eaters by force of circumstances when their food supply becomes depleted.

When people exercise proper dominion over animals and treat them with respect, the results can be heartwarming. A beloved animal may be viewed as a treasured companion, even as part of the family. The remarkable loyalty and devotion of animals actually causes some people to have stronger attachment and love for their pets than for some family members.

When you add up the different complex living creatures here on Earth, they number into the millions, with each acting as a unique book in a grand library of books just waiting to be studied. Each unique species must serve some purpose toward our needs. Already, we have gleaned vast amounts of valuable information, but much more remains yet unknown.

Every book has an author, a creator, as it were, who used his imagination to tell a story. The Creator of all the living creatures here on Earth has used superior imagination to provide man with a library filled with wonderful books of every sort imaginable for our enlightenment and joy.

SUPREME IMAGINATION

Progeny of an Intelligent, Reasoning Being

Though humankind was last to arrive on Earth, we represent the crowning glory of this garden planet, the shining jewel in the Universe. Humans were uniquely created with the ability to think and reason upon the majestic beauty bestowed upon this planet. They alone have an unending thirst for knowledge, they have studied and learned from the animals and can use their imagination to create music, art, architecture, and many other wonderful things. They alone reign supreme over all other life forms here in their dominion. Clearly, Earth and all other living things were designed for the benefit of humankind!

Of all the marvelous things on Earth, none is more astounding than the human brain. For example, every second some 100 million bits of information pour into the brain from the various senses. The human brain has been estimated to contain eighty or ninety billion non-neuronal cells as well as eighty or ninety billion neurons, of which about ten billion are cortical pyramidal cells. These cells pass signals to each other via as many as 1,000 trillion (one quadrillion) synaptic connections to make thinking, learning, and reasoning possible.

Picture yourself in this setting, where you awaken for the first time to find yourself immersed in lush green surroundings where you hear sounds of life all around you. Imagine how curious you would be as to where all these interesting sounds were coming from. What would be going through your mind as you looked upon a beautiful array of flowers and as you approached them you realize your sense of smell for the very first time? The senses you are experiencing rush over you and you want to experience more as you investigate further.

As you move farther forward in your delightful stroll you notice in a nearby tree a furry little creature you come to call a koala. As you carefully pull him from his perch and cuddle him in your arms you notice how his soft and furry skin feels different than yours, and how he responds to your cuddles as he snuggles against you as he feels safe and secure in your arms.

After you have placed him back in his tree, you notice some monkeys pulling bananas off a plant nearby and eating them. As you approach the tree, they curiously observe you as you, too, tear a banana from the tree and begin to eat it. But suddenly, you spit it out and throw it down to the ground—it was bitter. Then you notice the monkeys were peeling theirs first. You do the same and find the texture and taste very delightful and mouth-watering.

After eating some bananas with the monkeys, you feel dryness in your mouth; you are thirsty all of a sudden. In the near distance you hear the sound of rushing water. You approach its source; you notice a beautifully striped tiger and her young cubs downstream lapping up water. Getting closer, they seem indifferent to your presence; you, too, go down to the stream and scoop up some of the crystal-clear water to drink. You find that this satisfies your thirst and you are so content, sitting by the stream, playing with the tiger cubs—taking in all the new sensations.

Reflections of an Intelligent, Reasoning Being

As the day continues, your curiosity compels you to watch and play with the animals and experience their different personalities and mannerisms. You cannot help yourself; you must smell all the plants, especially the colorful ones. You delight in listening to the birds singing as you contemplate their melodious sounds.

As you come to a clearing you look up at the beautiful blue sky and puffy white clouds. You notice a couple of large birds gliding across the sky and you wonder to yourself: *How do they do that?* Then you follow the stream you drank from earlier toward a loud sound until you discover a cascading waterfall. As you walk under it, your whole body feels exhilarated as cool water rushes over you for the very first time. You think to yourself, *What a wonderful place this is!*

Later in the day, as the sun begins to set, you find yourself mesmerized by the many beautiful colors in the sky. As night falls you lay down on the soft green grass, to watch the sky darken. You are thrilled to witness for the first time the twinkling stars in the heavens. You notice a comet blazing across the sky and wonder where it came from and where it is going. As you lie there, at peace with the sound of creatures all around, you recall the thrilling experiences you have encountered for the first time that day. You reflect upon how excited you were to smell the flowers, and how it felt to cuddle with the little koala, how you learned by watching the monkeys, and how you watched the tigers drink from the stream, and how much fun you had playing with her cubs.

As you lie there, you think about what new experiences tomorrow will bring, and feel excited about the new things the animals will teach you. You ponder in awe at the vastness of the world that sparkles above you and wonder: How did I get here? What does it all mean? What is my purpose?—Why am I here? You feel an intense desire to know the answers to these questions. Like a young child, you wonder who will answer the questions that burn inside you.

In your final thoughts, you think of how beautiful, safe, and secure this place is and how delightful it would be if you could live in this beautiful garden forever. You roll over into the arms of your mate and the two of you slowly drift off to sleep.

Yes, as reasoning, intelligent humans we are unique among all other creatures here on Earth because we reflect in a small way the intelligence and imagination of our designer. We find ourselves uniquely suited to not only inhabit this planet but take care of it. If you could trade your life right now to live in this peaceful and tranquil setting would you do it? If you could escape from the crazy world we live in today, would you do it? Is this the way you imagine life should really be?

Our Little Ball of Cosmic Dust

It is a fact that an image is a mere reflection of the reality. As stated earlier, everything man has constructed, conceived, or devised has been a result of his imagination. Man's wonderful creative imagination is a **mere reflection** of the creative imagination that went into the design of the Universe; it is a testament to the Supreme Mind responsible for it all.

One cannot look at this photo of Earth from space and not wonder about our beginning and our incredible place in this Universe. We, alone in the Universe, have been gifted an imagination with the likeness of a Superior Architect who has demonstrated Supreme Imagination. Upon examining the most recent and sophisticated scientific evidence now coming forth, it becomes clear that He surely is responsible for our very existence. He alone has given us this special Jewel in the Universe, wonderfully prepared before our arrival. It is our home to take care of while our knowledge and wisdom grow as we learn more from the natural world around us.

Consider this for a moment: everything you see in this photo represents the entire existence of man. This is man's home. It was here, through Supreme Imagination, that man was formed from the ground and given the breath of life. Man, in likeness, has used his own imagination to create and conceive every invention, architectural structure, work of art, and every other material thing devised. This includes Hubble and Spitzer to capture these beautiful photos. It was all created, ironically, using the materials from the same ground that we were formed from. This Earth, in essence, is our ball of cosmic clay. We do not own the clay and we have created nothing that did not already exist here upon the Earth. We, ourselves, are merely living cosmic clay sculptures who have been permitted to take materials from the ground and sculpt them into whatever useful nonliving devices our imaginations can conceive. As man and woman, we have also been allowed to carry the gift of life and transfer the seeds of life to others. But this gift is not of our own making.

At some point, will we have the opportunity to explore our Awe-Inspiring Universe? The prospect of that is truly exciting, only time will tell. Who would have thought 400 years ago that man's imagination would lead him to the threshold of time and space to a world beyond anything he could have dreamed of? Man has peered back in time with flying space telescopes, developed by use of his imagination. He has discovered that there was Someone with an imagination far superior to his own. Someone who existed long before man arrived onto the scene. Someone who, billions of years ago, laid the foundations of this incredible universe we are just now discovering.

Have you ever pondered this question: *Who conceived this curious faculty we call Imagination?* Each of us has this intangible creative force within us to achieve anything we can imagine. The fact we can shape the world around us, is proof in and of itself of an original Creator who designed this creative force into us!

MAN'S IMAGINATION

Suicide by Carbon Monoxide Poison

While man has been given the gift of creative imagination, he has not always used it in a responsible way. He has too often devised things that have brought harm to his fellow man as well as the planet. Our planet Earth is a grand masterpiece worth preserving.

Suppose, as a parent, you spend many years imagining, designing, and constructing a beautiful home. And, after stocking it with food and everything that would be required to live comfortably, even some pets, you give it to your son and his wife as a gift. You ask for nothing in return except that they respect you and take good care of it as their family grows. Then you go away for awhile. Upon your return, you are disturbed as you approach because you see that smoke appears to be coming out of the house. You knock on the door, but no one answers.

As you make your way through the house, you notice that smoke fills the air, you find it hard to breathe, and it is uncomfortably warm. Your eyes are burning from the smoke. There seems to be trash thrown everywhere, there are spills that have ruined the carpet, and you begin to wonder, What have they done to this place?" They have ruined your beautiful home!

Over in the corner you notice a coal-burning stove that has no exhaust to the outside, and you think to yourself "How foolish of them to do that." Then you suddenly come to the realization that something is seriously wrong. As you rush through the house looking and calling out for your son and his family you are horrified to find all of them dead on the living room floor. They had each been overcome with carbon monoxide poison. What a senseless and avoidable tragedy.

For a brief moment turn back to the setting on page 102 and look at the condition the earth was in when man first inherited it. The air was pure, the water crystal clear, and the land was covered with lush green vegetation. Now look at the image on this page and ponder the contrast between the two settings. Do you see a larger, far more serious parallel to the illustration above that threatens life on this planet?

The World Health Organization reports that 3 million people now die each year from the effects of air pollution. This is three times the 1 million who die each year in automobile accidents. Air pollutants include carbon monoxide, ozone, sulfur dioxide, nitrogen oxides, and particulates. These pollutants come primarily from the combustion of fossil fuels, principally coal-fired power plants and gasoline-powered automobiles. Is it too late to avoid the inevitable tragedy that awaits the human race? Have we already passed the tipping point?

Should we not pause for a moment and think about what we are doing to this planet—our home? Are you concerned there is no exhaust for the pollution we are creating? Could man's imagination be used in a better way? Will we one day be caretakers of countless other planets throughout the Universe? If so, we are off to a bumpy start!

Oh what a paradise this earth would be, if it weren't for selfish humanity.

Power Beyond Comprehension

To whom will you compare me? Who is my equal?

Power Beyond Comprehension

Each day when we wake up we take for granted that the sun will rise in the east and shower us with its rays of life-giving energy. Without our Sun, life simply would not exist here on Earth. Yet when you take a closer look at the makeup of it you have to wonder why we don't simply burn up from its intense heat.

Our solar system's star, the Sun, has inspired mythological stories in cultures around the world, including those of the ancient Egyptians, the Aztecs of Mexico, Native American tribes of North America and Canada, the Chinese, and many others. A number of ancient cultures built stone structures or modified natural rock formations to observe the Sun and Moon. They charted the seasons, created calendars, and monitored solar and lunar eclipses. These architectural sites show evidence of deliberate alignment to astronomical phenomena: sunrises, moonrises, moonsets, even stars or planets.

The **Sun** is the star at the center of our solar system, and is currently traveling through the Local Interstellar Cloud in the Local Bubble zone, within the inner rim of the Orion Arm of the Milky Way galaxy. It has a circumference of about 2,715,364 miles, about 111 times that of Earth at 24,873 miles. The Sun's mass (about 332,900 times that of Earth) accounts for about 99.86% of the total mass of the solar system. The core temperature of the Sun is close to 27,000,000 degrees Fahrenheit. It is, on average, about ninety-three million miles from the Earth. Yet, on a sunny day, its heat can blister your skin. Stare at it long enough and you would go blind! Remarkably, only about one billionth of the Sun's energy strikes the Earth. Still, this fraction of the Sun's power is enough to sustain life on the planet.

The Sun, like most stars, is a main sequence star, and thus generates its energy by nuclear fusion of hydrogen nuclei into helium. In its core, the Sun fuses 620 million metric tons of hydrogen each second. The Sun's hot corona continuously expands in space, creating the solar wind, a stream of charged particles that extends to the heliopause at roughly 100 astronomical units (one astronomical unit is equal to about 92,955,807.27 miles).

Scientists have calculated that the total energy output from just our Sun is enough to sustain some 31 trillion planets like the Earth. To measure this enormous output another way: If all the Sun's power could be harnessed for just one second, it would provide the United States with enough energy, at its current usage rate, for the next 9,000,000 years.

As mind-numbing and awe-inspiring as the extreme energy our Sun produces each second is, it is in reality a relatively small sun among the countless trillions of other stars in the Universe. Compared to the red hypergiant star VY Canis Majoris located in the constellation Canis Major (with an estimated circumference of 5.2 billion miles), our Sun is but a speck of dust in the grand scheme of things.

Mercury < Mars < Venus < Earth

Earth < Neptune < Uranus < Saturn < Jupiter

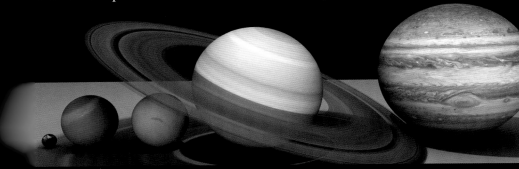

Jupiter < Wolf 359 < Sun < Sirius

Putting Things Into Perspective

When we put things into perspective, it is truly humbling. It forces us to realize how puny and insignificant we really are. It begs the question: How can we, mere specs of dust, question the existence of the One responsible for all these stars?

Who among us could compare themselves to any of these dynamic star powerhouses of energy sprinkled throughout the Universe like perfectly cut diamonds? How could we challenge the Creator who brought them forth with vigorous power?

By studying and thinking about the images in this chart to the left and on the following pages, you will no doubt have an awakened sense of smallness and humility. Especially since these stars represent only a tiny slice of the cosmic web, with countless trillions of trillions of stars that compose the universe. The point of this exercise is to help you understand how incomprehensibly powerful is the energy unleashed in the Universe. May it drive home the point that Isaiah spoke an unfathomable truth.

Starting with Mercury and ending with Earth, notice in the first section how the size of things gets progressively larger, but how Earth is dwarfed by Jupiter in the second section, then notice how Jupiter is dwarfed by the star Sirius in the third section. Sirius is known in the night sky as the Dog star reflecting its prominence in its constellation, Canis Major (Big Dog), the sky's brightest star. Its brightness makes it easy to find on winter and spring evenings. To the early Greeks, the season following the star's appearance came to be known as the Dog Days of summer.

Circumference Size Comparison Chart

Mercury	9,525 mi
Mars	13,259 mi
Venus	23,627 mi
Earth	24,873 mi
Neptune	96,683 mi
Uranus	99,787 mi
Saturn	235,297 mi
Jupiter	279,118 mi
Wolf 359	434,458 mi
Sun	2,715,364 mi
Sirius	5,231,615 mi

Giants Among Us

Sirius < Pollux < Arcturus < Aldebaran

Aldebaran < Rigel < Antares < Betelgeuse

Betelgeuse < Mu Cephei < VV Cephei A < VY Canis Majoris

Super Stars Beyond Belief

When we think things just could not get any bigger, the Hubble Telescope seems to defy our imagination by presenting another star larger than its predecessors.

While the exact size of these super stars is sometimes in question among scientists, the masses listed in these tables are inferred from theory, using difficult measurements of the stars' temperatures and their absolute brightness but one thing is clear: as our knowledge grows and the technology improves, our sense of awe increases with each new find.

As you saw on the previous page, Sirius dwarfed everything in our solar system. Starting with Sirius and ending with Aldebaran on the top page to the left, notice in the first section here how the size of celestial bodies again gets progressively larger. Sirius (which dwarfed Jupiter on the preceeding page) is dwarfed by Aldebaran, and how Aldebaran is dwarfed by Betelgeuse in the second section.

Betelgeuse is classified as a red supergiant, and is one of the largest and most luminous stars known. If it was at the center of our solar system, its surface would extend past the asteroid belt possibly to the orbit of Jupiter and beyond, wholly engulfing Mercury, Venus, Earth, and Mars.

Now notice in the third section at the bottom, how Betelgeuse is dwarfed by VY Canis Majoris in the final section. VY Canis Majoris is a red hypergiant star, located in the constellation Canis Major in the Milky Way galaxy. It is currently the largest known star by volume and also one of the most luminous yet discovered. It is located about 4,900 light-years from Earth, and dwarfs them all making our Sun just a speck next to it and Earth invisible as you will see on the next page!

Circumference Size Comparison Chart

Sirius	5,231,615 mi
Pollux	26,665,620 mi
Arcturus	61,295,788 mi
Aldebaran	120,019,088 mi
Rigel	185,449,041 mi
Antares	1,494,524,060 mi
Betelgeuse	1,902,121,540 mi
MU Cephei	3,260,779,780 mi
VV Cephei A	4,755,303,840 mi
VY Canis Majoris	5,298,767,140 mi

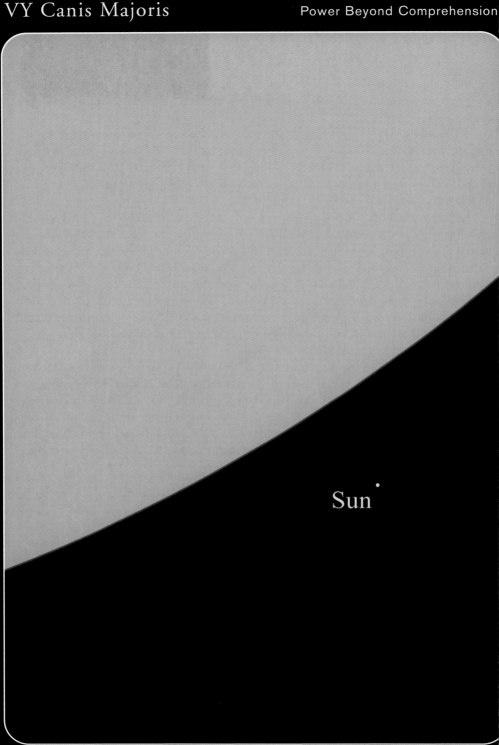

Sun

To Whom Can You Compare Me

To put things into a perspective we can wrap our minds around consider this: our Sun, seen as a tiny dot to the left, is 332,900 times more massive than Earth (Earth is not visible here) but the volume of the star VY Canis Majoris is so incredibly vast, it would take 7 quadrillion Earths to fill the volume. While the circumference of VY Canis Majoris is a staggering distance of 5.2 billion miles it is but a dot within the Milky Way galaxy which has an approximate diameter of 600 quadrillion miles with a circumference of 1,884,000,000,000,000,000 miles (1.8 quintillion miles) made up of billions of stars.

The Milky Way galaxy is just one of over 125 billion galaxies in the known universe but, in the grand scale of things it is only a dot in the observable universe which has a diameter of what is commonly thought to be 93 billion light-years. That would be a calculated distance of 93,000,000,000 x 6,000,000,000,000 = 558,000,000,000,000,000,000,000 miles (558 Sextillion miles) or a circumference of approximately 1.7 septillion miles, a number beyond the author's comprehension.

Astronomers, with the help of the Hubble Space Telescope, have predicted that VY Canis Majoris will be blown up, as a hypernova, in less than 100,000 years. A hypernova is an explosion with an energy burst of over 100 supernovae. Supernovae are extremely luminous and cause a burst of radiation that often briefly outshines an entire galaxy, before fading from view over several weeks or months. During this short interval a single supernova can radiate as much energy as the Sun is expected to emit over 10 billion years.

VY Canis Majoris is the elephant in the room for those who would deny the simple truths in the words penned by Isaiah. This simple man had no knowledge of astronomy, science, or any Earthly concept of the incredible universe beyond the night sky of his day. Nevertheless, he spoke of the incomparable power and dynamic energy of his God whom he believed created all the stars, calling each by name.

We are each faced with an undeniable truth, whether we want to admit it or not. While Isaiah's words were not scientific, they do underscore this scientific fact: the Hubble telescope has uncovered a divine truth uttered long ago that there simply is no equal in power to the One who created all the stars. *To whom can you compare me? Who is my equal?*

How could Isaiah gain access to such scientifically accurate information about this incomprehensible energy source some 2,700 years before it was revealed by the Hubble Telescope? There is one logical explanation. The One with the power and wisdom to create the heavens and the Earth could certainly give Isaiah such advanced insight. This gives weight to the Bible's claim that it is "inspired of God."

Hubble Reveals Creation

Look at this image to the left and reflect upon the images and data on the preceding pages. This will give you a sense of Awe and a sense of reality of what Hubble has captured over the last two decades. As it orbits high above the Earth, it has been filming the grandest drama in human history. It has recorded the creation of an Awe-Inspiring Universe. It is an undeniable truth that an incomparable, Awe-Inspiring Power is the source of it all.

Hubble has peered back 13.7 billion years to capture the beginning of time and space as we have come to understand it. It recorded evidence of an organized explosion of energy on a scale incomprehensible to the human mind. Like a single cosmic seed planted in the rich soil of dark energy, Hubble has witnessed an explosive growth of stars as they reproduced and clustered into island galaxies like grape clusters on a vine.

As the Universe expanded into a symphony of galaxies, as though directed by a Grand Conductor, it expanded at an exponential rate, much like a vineyard of grapes would grow as it aged. In amongst those galaxies a special galaxy called the Milky Way formed that gave birth to a special star, our Sun. From the dust lanes of the Sun, the planet we call Earth formed from star dust with all the ingredients for life built within, lacking only the breath of life.

As vegetation abounded, Earth's atmosphere developed, and an endless variety of life emerged, each reproducing according to their respective kinds. Sea life emerged in colorful variety in all the oceans and bodies of water. Following sea life, flying creatures of every size and form sprang up as each took flight into the sky. Then land-dwelling animals of every description emerged to roam the land. Finally, the crowning glory of living creatures made its appearance here on Earth; intelligent humans sculpted from clay were given the breath of life to reign supreme over all other Earthly life forms—as caretakers of their home called Earth!

As we review the evidence Hubble has discovered, we see the orderly process of how the Universe developed. Stars multiplied and clustered into galaxies. We see how the Earth formed with meticulous preparation to support intelligent life. It becomes obvious to the reasoning mind that this is no accident. This is the work of a Grand Architect with Supreme Imagination who had a purpose in mind: to crown this Grand Work with intelligent human beings as his PROGENY.

Like a child without a parent, we would be without a Creator. No child has ever experienced life without someone to provide them with life. Life can only come from life, it's that simple! Those who would deny this simple truth choose to ignore this basic fact.

Look at this image and as you gaze out into this vast Universe just imagine what the future may hold. Look at Hubble and think of the wealth of knowledge we are gleaning as a result of our imagination. Look at the Earth and see how beautiful it is just floating in dark space and how it may be only the beginning of our journey into this Awe-Inspiring universe!

Creative Imagination

What a Wonderful, Intangible Force!

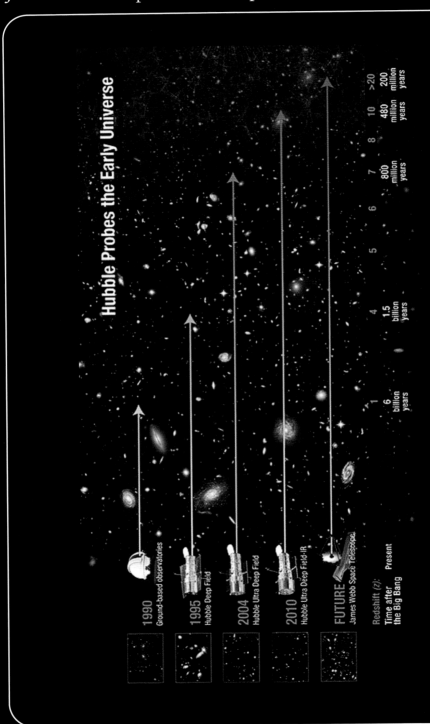

Today's Dream is Tomorrow's Reality

When Galileo turned his newly improved telescope to the night sky, he found a doorway that no one before him had discovered. With his discovery he had cracked the door open just enough to get a glimpse of a world he had never imagined. In March 1610, Galileo published the first scientific treatise based on observations made through a telescope. He called it *The Starry Messenger*. The question one must now ponder is this: was Galileo, unbeknownst to himself, merely the first character in a string of characters to act out his role in a pre-scripted 400-year rehearsal? This rehearsal has culminated in filming the greatest drama in human history. With the telescope, Galileo ignited a Scientific Revolution in the study of the night sky. It revealed phenomena in the heavens that Aristotle and others had not dreamed of. It had a profound influence on the controversy of an Earth-centered universe in his day.

In the generations since the seventeenth century, astronomers and scientists had managed to pry that door open a little wider with improvements to the telescope. It was not until the twentieth century that the door was flung wide open with the invention of flying telescopes, like the Hubble and later, the Spitzer. Soon to come will be the James Webb Next Generation telescope, which will be far more powerful than the Hubble.

The JWST will be a true successor to the Hubble Space Telescope (HST) in that it will be able to see many more and much older stars. Its primary mirror has a collecting area which is almost six times larger than the HTS. The JWST's primary scientific mission has four main components: to search for light from the first stars and galaxies which formed in the Universe after the Big Bang, to study the formation of galaxies, to understand the formation of stars and planetary systems, and to study planetary systems and the origins of life. It is expected to look back within 180,000 years of the Big Bang and can be compared to a seventy-year-old person looking back in time and seeing themselves as an eleven-month-old baby. (This chart shows how man's depth of sight into the Universe is picking up its pace every few years now, instead of decades as in the past.)

Here are some key questions to ponder: What new technology will our imaginations create in the future that seems impossible today, but will become tomorrow's reality? Like bees spreading pollen from plant-to-plant to keep the miracle of life growing, will man someday go from planet-to-planet, galaxy-to-galaxy, spreading the miracle of life throughout the Universe? Is it man's eternal purpose to transform the cosmos into a beautiful world, full of life as we grow and expand our imagination? Can you imagine being a part of something so Grand? Just imagine how thrilling it would be!

Imagination is the key. As Einstein stated, "Imagination is everything. If we could just use it only for good and not for bad, what a world this would be!" Come on World—Use your Imagination—for Good!

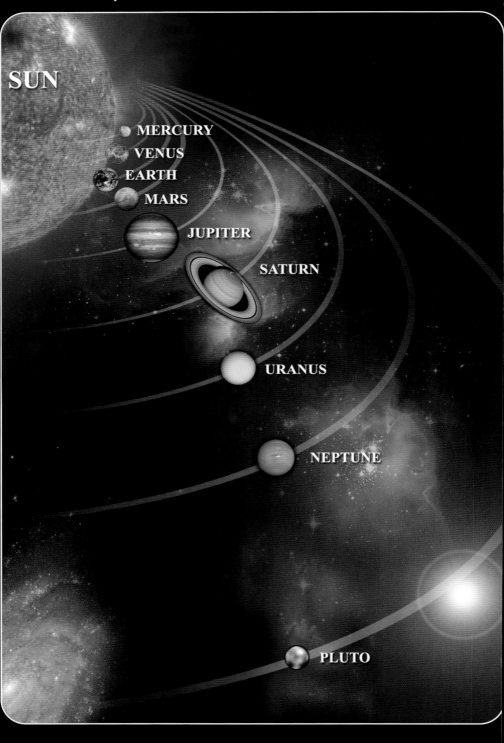

SUN

MERCURY

VENUS

EARTH

MARS

JUPITER

SATURN

URANUS

NEPTUNE

PLUTO

SUPREME IMAGINATION

In the Stream of Time

Where are we? In the stream of time, that is. In man's best estimations, the Universe as we know it from our vantage point is around 13.7 billion years old. Our Milky Way galaxy is thought to be 13.2 billion years old. Our Sun is considered to be 4.6 billion years old. The Earth began to form shortly thereafter, about 4.54 billion years ago.

According to the Big Bang theory, this Grand Universe we have just begun to discover through the use of our collective imaginations was conceived in 1 Plank unit of time. It resulted from some sort of subatomic seed compacted with dynamic energy of an unknown nature, completely incomprehensible to man. Thus far, the theory has proven congruent with evidence from Hubble. At the moment of conception, germination, or whatever term you want to use short of miracle, a Grand Universe was born which has blossomed forth, stars without number, collecting into massive black holes to become the central powerhouse for galaxies that, in turn, have given birth to billions of other stars, who, in their turn, have birthed planets and other cosmic phenomenon.

The all-inclusive *incomparable energy* that powers all the heavenly bodies in the Universe is a power beyond man's ability to understand. The only term in our human vocabulary that can come close to describing it is *Supernatural* or *God-like*.

Regardless of one's personal beliefs or religious convictions, this *scientific fact* gives us reason to consider the implications of Isaiah's ancient statement.

The outgrowth of matter from the early universe led to the formation of our solar system, where we now find ourselves some 13.7 billion years later. As caretakers of a planet 4.54 billion years old, with a recorded human history of just over 5,500 years, we have just begun our journey. We are but babes in the grand stream of time.

Where do we go from here? We are physical beings in a physical universe perfectly suited for us; but we struggle to know why we are here. In many ways, we are being tested on our ability to respect and manage this gift we call Earth. Only through using our collective imaginations— for good all the time and for the benefit of all—can we go forward and finish the work we have to do on Earth before moving on to countless other planets in the cosmos. To mankind, the universe including the earth is like a gift from a parent to a child. It's like a wonderful fun-filled book full of adventure and mystery that educates and intrigues us the more we peer into and study it. What a wonderful book!

The Designer of the planets in our solar system and across the Universe surely had a Grand Purpose in mind for them and us when we were placed right in the middle of it all. Now, that vexing question: *Where are we in the stream of time?* Right where we are supposed to be, at the beginning of a wonderful journey, a journey of adventure where our imaginations will likely compel us to go forward by some future means into an amazing universe, *made just for us*, in our quest for knowledge and a sense of purpose and meaning to life!

Imagine—A Perfect World!

If you could imagine a perfect world, what would it look like? Perhaps this world is what you would envision.

Imagine—an Earth with no holes in the ozone where poisonous radiation is pouring in to harm you. There are no clouds of smoke and poisonous gases spewing from smokestacks or motorized vehicles. There are no global warming issues to worry about because the environment is perfect. The air we breathe is clean and pure once again, with no more smog. You can see the stars clearly when you look up at the night sky. The polar ice caps are stable and no longer in danger of melting. There are no harsh climate conditions caused by unnatural and accelerated global changes.

Imagine—the world's oceans have been cleaned up from all the pollution that has been dumped into them. The water is crystal clear once again, no more murky water to swim in. The coral reefs have all been restored to their original beautiful condition. There is no more red tide or other conditions that kill sea life. All the species once near extinction are flourishing again. The oceans are teeming with an ideal balance of sea creatures of every kind. Dolphins and other fish are no longer caught up in nets, nor do they die from consuming plastic and other waste left by humans. No oil spills. The water in all the lakes and rivers is crystal clear and pollution-free. To drink it, all you have to do is reach down and scoop it up with your hands.

Imagine—if man were suddenly removed from the Earth, the Earth's self-cleansing process would kick-in immediately and dramatically. Eventually, over time, the air, lakes, rivers, oceans, and the global environment would be pure and clean once again.

Imagine that. Man is the problem! How did things get this way? IMAGINA-TION—man's selfish misuse of it! It can all be reversed when all humans learn to use their IMAGINATION unselfishly to the benefit of their fellowman!

Imagine—a world where there are no more wars. Everyone is living in peace. No mothers, fathers, brothers, sisters, wives, husbands, or children have to mourn the loss of loved ones on the battlefield. No more innocent children maimed or killed from landmines. No more threat of nuclear bombs. No more tanks, missiles, or poisonous gas. In fact, there is no longer a need for weapons because all humans respect each other and treat one another like brothers and sisters. Everyone is kind and considerate to each other. The world is a place where we serve one another rather than ourselves. There is no more racial strife or national hatred because all are considered equals. No more political discord or corrupt leaders. There is no more religious conflict or indifference because the world's spirituality is singular.

Imagine—a world where cancer has been cured, heart disease is no more, HIV is a thing of the past. No more blindness, no need for hearing aids, no need for wheelchairs. No more mental illness. Hospitals close down—no more patients, so doctors are unnecessary as well. No one gets sick anymore, that is a thing of the past. There are no more tombstones or graveyards; the dead loved ones you longed for have returned. You get up each day feeling youthful, full of vitality and energy, ready to see what exciting adventures the day will bring.

Imagine—a world where no one is mugged, robbed, or raped. Where children can play safely and not worry about being abducted or molested. There are no drive-by shootings or murders. You don't have to lock your doors because no one will rob you or steal your things. There are no bullies to pick on you or make fun of you. There are no homeless, or children without parents. You do not have to be afraid to walk down a dark street alone, because there is no one to harm you. There are no wives or husbands suffering from spousal abuse. There are no more prisons, because there are no more criminals. There are no more drunk drivers to kill and maim innocent people. No more homes broken from divorce.

Imagine—a world where there is no more famine, no more hunger. There are no children with bloated stomachs dying from malnutrition. There is plenty of nutritious food for everyone to eat. There is an abundant variety and it is all delicious. There is plenty of clean water to drink.

Imagine—there are no more zoos, because the animals roam free. There is no need to cage them because they will not harm you. There are no more animals being senselessly killed. Once endangered animals thrive once again. Children can play with all the animals and not be bitten, mauled, or harmed in any way.

Imagine—a world where the work you do is not drudgery, but a delight, because it is the job of your dreams—your passion. You love your job as a marine biologist, an artist, an entertainer, an astronomer, a musician, a gourmet cook, a teacher, an engineer, or an architect—or all of the above, because time is endless for you. You travel the world and see all there is to see. You take time as you travel to meet every other person on the planet and spend time getting to know them. You love animals, so you take the time to study and learn all there is to know about every animal on the planet. You take the time to explore the oceans and get to know about every single sea creature.

Imagine—a world where the Earth is a base station; the starting point from where human life is eventually spread out into the endless and timeless universe. In this world our collective imagination is used only for the good and benefit of all, and to devise and create previously unimagined means to travel the universe. It is a world where, through the use of imagination, we become caretakers of the worlds beyond this doorway, to populate, beautify, and maintain for eternity with a complete sense of purpose and reverence for the one responsible for it all!

Through Imagination we discovered this doorway to a world without boundaries, and a drama of creation beyond our wildest dreams. Can our imagination now be used to bring us a perfect world that will spread throughout the Universe for all eternity? Our first step to this reality is Imagination. Only when all of Earth's inhabitants can imagine a perfect world, will it become a reality! You may say "this is an unrealistic world." In reality this world reflects basic human desires. Who in their right mind would not want to live in the world just described? *"With men this is impossible, but with God all things are possible."*— **Jesus Christ**

Only if you can Imagine it; will it be yours! So go ahead and imagine it!

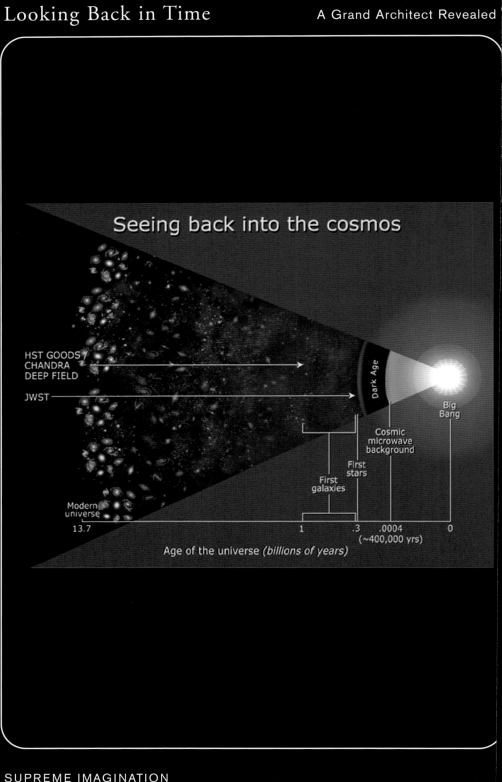

What Does It All Mean?

What can we conclude? What does it all mean? Is there a bigger picture for us to see? Since truth is that which conforms to fact or reality, to answer those questions we must look at the facts. From what we have discovered beyond this doorway, the evidence is clear that there exists an incomparable power source that has created all the stars, just as the ancient prophet Isaiah stated long before the telescope was invented. The evidence is also clear that nothing comes into existence devoid of imagination.

This incomparable power source is beyond our comprehension, though it is not beyond our imagination. Even though it is beyond our comprehension that this power source surely has always existed, that, too, is not beyond our imagination. As humans, we possess an imagination that serves as the driving force we use to create and shape our future and envision life's coming attractions. This is a simple truth—our existence and the universe around us could only have come about through the same process of imagination but from an entity with a vastly superior sense of imagination (Imagination Supreme).

We can trust that the Genesis account had it right; the universe had a beginning just as Hubble discovered, as evident in the Big Bang (see image to left). While leaving out the fine details, it turns out the Genesis account of creation, also gave us an accurate overview as to how Earth was formed in its early stages, shrouded in darkness. Spitzer has discovered that in Sun-like star systems planets are formed in lanes of dense dust corresponding to Genesis 1:2 (see pages 82 to 88). Then Hubble and Spitzer together revealed with the Sun-like star called HD 107146, that as planets mature the dense dust is polished away to where the Sun's light would gradually filter through, making day and night distinguishable, corresponding with Genesis 1:3 (see page 90). We do not have full comprehension of any of these acts of Supreme Creative Imagination. However, little by little we are getting the details with telescopes like Hubble, Spitzer and soon the JWST which will no doubt give us additional details the Genesis account left out about this Awe-Inspiring event in its basic explanation of creation.

Think about how we each use our creative imagination to envision, create, and bring into existence things that which formerly did not exist. Your vision of your future creation, be it a painting, an invention, a book, a song, or whatever, starts as a thought process and through the use of your imagination you devise a way to bring your vision into reality. Now, that product or creation can never come into existence on its own. It will not create itself. You have to imagine it. You have to create it. You, alone, have to make it a reality—it simply will not come about any other way.

Like the creation or product conceived in your mind, the Universe even though gravity, electromagnetism, and other forces, not fully understood are at work, it could never have come into existence on its own, it could not create itself. Someone with an incomprehensible power and Supreme Imagination had to first envision and imagine it, and then they had to create these forces and set them into motion and make it a reality. Even though none of us witnessed the invention of fireworks, it does not discard the facts that someone with imagination took raw energy in the form of gun powder and turned it into a beautiful display of energy. We have the evidence.

Even though we did not witness the creation of the Universe, it does not alter the fact that someone with Supreme Imagination did it. Scientist cannot just throw this faculty of imagination out the window and say the Universe created itself under the force of gravity. That would just raise the question "where did the gravity come from"? We have the evidence now, pouring in from space via flying telescopes of a Grand Architect of Superior Design that gives evidence of Supreme Imagination. As time marches on, this body of evidence will continue to mount with each generation as we further our quest to know, through the use of imagination.

As we now witness this Grand Drama unfold before us, the evidence, the facts, and the reality lead to this important conclusion: What Isaiah must have envisioned on that starry night as he looked up into the heavens and pondered the profound words he wrote, is that those words are an UNFATHOMABLE DIVINE TRUTH."

How could Isaiah gain access to such scientifically accurate information about this incomprehensible energy source some 2,700 years before it was revealed by the Hubble Telescope? There is one logical explanation. Someone who knew the details of creation had to reveal it to him.

Some scientists have long debated that the Genesis account of creation is wrong and that the proof is in the science. Can such scientists ignore this fact: Hubble and Spitzer have now discovered that Genesis, in simple language revealed the accurate science of it long before science came into existence?

Those who fail to recognize the significance of this Grand Drama are missing out on a historic event of universal proportions. This event has given humanity a golden opportunity to peer into the mind of Supreme Imagination. What Hubble has discovered takes us to the edge of time and the beginning of a Grand Creation that has led to our very existence. It is giving us a glimpse at a power beyond human comprehension that is humbling to those who understand the source of this power.

Have we, perhaps, been drawn to this Doorway by the One who created all the stars in order to show us His incomparable power and Imagination? Is there a bigger purpose He wants to show us—beyond this Earth—to expand our imagination forever? Can we say for a certainty that the insatiable quest to the stars man embarked upon with the invention of the telescope and the race it sparked, costing tens of billions of dollars and hundreds of millions of man-hours has been of man's own doing? Have those engaged in this quest been mere characters among a string of cast members performing their part as they each were drawn along by some invisible and compelling force to lead us to this Grand Revelation? Only time will tell!

Just as with any stage drama, there are many things that go on behind the scenes that make the production work, things the audience never sees. Likewise with the Universe, there are obviously things going on behind the scenes of the visible universe that we cannot see nor understand for now.

Like wide-eyed children we now find ourselves seated in the theater of imagination in awe of every scene as each inspiring frame is transmitted from space to complete the reel of this silent motion picture. We don't fully comprehend for now what is unfolding on the screen before us, or what it all means, because the drama is not yet over and there are still many scenes yet to come.

As man is drawn forward into the future by his insatiable quest for knowledge and a sense of purpose, the pieces to life's puzzle will come together, and as the big picture emerges, he will finally understand his purpose in this vast and wonderful Universe he has just discovered and recognize that it is all a product of an Intelligent Designer with Supreme Imagination of a DIVINE NATURE—To Whom We Owe Our Very Existence!

We are but toddlers in a Grand and Infinite Universe on an insatiable quest for understanding!

THE GALLERY

OF A FORMERLY UNKNOWN ARTIST
WITH SUPREME IMAGINATION

The Gallery of Supreme Art

On the following pages you will view the artwork of the Grandest Artist ever known, whose works, until recently, were unknown! It is truly out of this world and a grand reflection of Supreme Power, Wisdom, Artistic Genius, and Creative Imagination—beyond human comprehension. These works of cosmic art tell a story of our past, including the creation of man's existence on Earth.

How did these Heavenly works of art come about? Common logic dictates that, as with any great work of art, imagination played a key role; in this case, Supreme Imagination had to have been used. And it required expended effort and energy on the part of the designer—in this case, Dynamic Energy beyond belief.

These works of art were not painted by mere mortals with brush strokes of colored oil paints onto cloth canvases. No, they were painted with cosmic dust supercharged with dynamic energy onto a canvas of dark energy peppered with stars covering billions of light-years across the great expanse of the heavens—truly a living orchestra playing in symphony.

In likeness of this Supreme Architect, man has been given the wonderful gift of creative imagination and, thus, we can now view this exquisite collection through space telescopes, like an unfolding Drama, perhaps in response to that invitation from 2,700 years ago. No other generation has been given such a peek into the mind of such Supreme Imagination. Realize, that as beautiful as these images are, they are mere reflections of the reality that are alive, in motion, and powered by dynamic energy. This collection is living proof of their Designer's Superior Power, Design, Wisdom, and Imagination.

Hopefully this gallery will inspire you, build your appreciation, and reaffirm your conviction for the Supreme Imagination demonstrated by the One responsible for these heavenly works of art. Each accompanying page contains information about the image. Also, for a comparison, at the bottom of each page are the names of men and women who have been respected for what they achieved through the use of their creative imaginations and the contributions they made to help shape our small world.

As you look at the awe-inspiring images on the left, compare the creative difference between them and the manmade inventions listed below the text. You will no doubt agree that as creative and important as man's accomplishments are, they pale in comparison to the Supreme Imagination behind these wonderful cosmic works.

"Imagination is everything."

How will we use this curious faculty to shape our future?

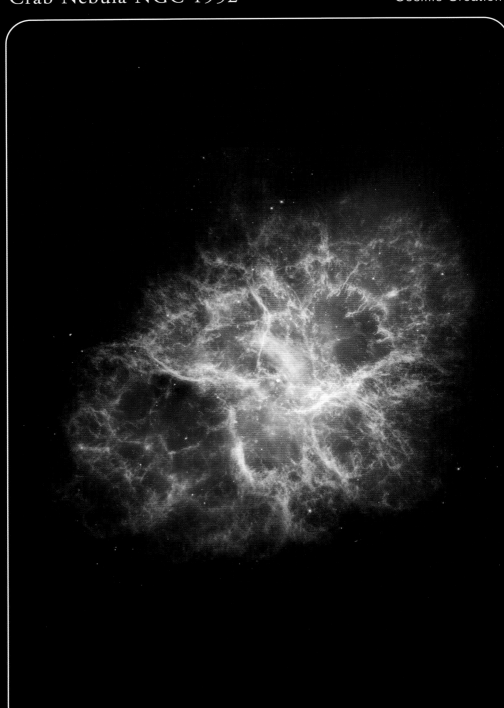

Crab Nebula NGC 1952

This is a mosaic image, one of the largest ever taken by NASA's Hubble Space Telescope of the Crab Nebula, a six-light-year-wide expanding remnant of a star's supernova explosion. Japanese and Chinese astronomers recorded this violent event nearly 1,000 years ago in 1054, as did, almost certainly, Native Americans.

The orange filaments are the tattered remains of the star and consist mostly of hydrogen. The rapidly spinning neutron star embedded in the center of the nebula is the dynamo powering the nebula's eerie interior bluish glow. The blue light comes from electrons whirling at nearly the speed of light around magnetic field lines from the neutron star. The neutron star, like a lighthouse, ejects twin beams of radiation that appear to pulse thirty times a second due to the neutron star's rotation. A neutron star is the crushed ultra-dense core of the exploded star.

The Crab Nebula derived its name from its appearance in a drawing made by Irish astronomer Lord Rosse in 1844, using a 36-inch telescope. When viewed by Hubble, as well as by large ground-based telescopes such as the European Southern Observatory's Very Large Telescope, the Crab Nebula takes on a more detailed appearance that yields clues into the spectacular demise of a star 6,500 light-years away.

This composite image of the Crab Nebula uses data from three of NASA's Great Observatories. The Chandra X-ray image is shown in light blue, the Hubble Space Telescope optical images are in green and dark blue, and the Spitzer Space Telescope's infrared image is in red. The size of the X-ray image is smaller than the others because the outwardly streaming higher-energy electrons emitting X-ray light radiate away their energy more quickly than the lower-energy electrons emitting optical and infrared light. The neutron star, which has the mass equivalent to the sun crammed into a rapidly spinning ball of neutrons twelve miles across, is the bright-white dot in the center of the image.

The matter from a neutron star is so dense that one teaspoon of matter can weigh as much as 200 million elephants.

Imagination of Man

Great Pyramid of Cheops ~ Egyptian Pharaoh Khufu of the Fourth Dynasty

Stars Bursting to Life in the Chaotic Carina Nebula

This image of a huge pillar of star birth composed of gas and dust resides in a tempestuous stellar nursery called the **Carina Nebula**, located 7,500 light-years away in the southern constellation Carina. This image, taken in visible light, shows the tip of the three-light-year-long pillar bathed in the glow of light from hot, massive stars off the top of the image. Scorching radiation and fast winds (streams of charged particles) from these stars are sculpting the pillar and causing new stars to form within it. Streamers of gas and dust can be seen flowing off the top of the structure.

Nestled inside this dense structure are fledgling stars. They cannot be seen in this image because they are hidden by a wall of gas and dust. Although the stars themselves are invisible, one of them is providing evidence of its existence. Thin puffs of material can be seen traveling to the left and to the right of a dark notch in the center of the pillar. The matter is part of a jet produced by a young star. Farther away, on the left, the jet is visible as a grouping of small wispy clouds. A few small clouds are visible at a similar distance on the right side of the jet. Astronomers estimate that the jet is moving at speeds of up to 850,000 miles an hour. The jet's total length is about ten light-years.

With its Wide Field Camera 3 (WFC3) aboard, the Hubble Telescope extends from ultraviolet to visible to infrared light. By penetrating the wall of gas and dust, the infrared vision of WFC3 reveals infant stars because infrared light, unlike visible light, can pass through the dust.

Surrounding the stellar nursery is a treasure chest full of stars, most of which cannot be seen in the visible-light image because dense gas clouds veil their light. Many of them are background stars.

Hubble's Wide Field Camera 3 observed the Carina Nebula on July 24-30, 2009. WFC3 was installed aboard Hubble in May 2009 during Servicing Mission 4. The composite image was made from filters that isolate emission from iron, magnesium, oxygen, hydrogen, and sulfur.

Imagination of Man

Microprocessor ~ Ted Hoff, Jr.
(1971)

Star Formation in RCW49

One of the most prolific birthing grounds in our Milky Way galaxy, a nebula called RCW 49 is exposed in superb detail for the first time in this new image from NASA's Spitzer Space Telescope. Located 13,700 light-years away in the southern constellation Centaurus, RCW 49 is a dark and dusty stellar nursery that houses more than 2,200 stars.

Because many of the stars in RCW 49 are deeply embedded in plumes of dust, they cannot be seen at visible wavelengths. When viewed with Spitzer's infrared eyes, however, RCW 49 becomes transparent. Like cracking open a quartz rock to discover its jewels inside, the nebula's newborn stars have been dramatically exposed.

This image taken by Spitzer's infrared array camera highlights the nebula's older stars (blue stars in center pocket), its gas filaments (green), and dusty tendrils (pink). Speckled throughout the murky clouds are more than 300 never-before-seen newborn stars.

Astronomers are interested in further studying these newfound proto-stars because they offer a fresh look at star formation in our own galaxy.

Imagination of Man

Negative/Positive Photographic Process ~ William Tabot
(1840)

Whirlpool Galaxy M51 and Companion Galaxy

The graceful winding arms of the majestic spiral galaxy M51 (NGC 5194) appear like a grand spiral staircase sweeping through space. They are actually long lanes of stars and gas laced with dust. This sharpest-ever image of the Whirlpool Galaxy, taken in January 2005 with the Advanced Camera for Surveys aboard NASA's Hubble Space Telescope, illustrates a spiral galaxy's grand design, from its curving spiral arms, where young stars reside, to its yellowish central core, a home of older stars. The galaxy is nicknamed the Whirlpool because of its swirling structure.

The Whirlpool's most striking feature is its two curving arms, a hallmark of so-called grand-design spiral galaxies. Many spiral galaxies possess numerous loosely shaped arms which make their spiral structure less pronounced. These arms serve an important purpose in spiral galaxies. They are star-formation factories, compressing hydrogen gas and creating clusters of new stars. In the Whirlpool, the assembly line begins with the dark clouds of gas on the inner edge, then moves to bright-pink star-forming regions, and ends with the brilliant-blue star clusters along the outer edge.

Some astronomers believe that the Whirlpool's arms are so prominent because of the effects of a close encounter with NGC 5195, the small yellowish galaxy at the outermost tip of one of the Whirlpool's arms. At first glance, the compact galaxy appears to be tugging on the arm. Hubble's clear view, however, shows that NGC 5195 is passing behind the Whirlpool. The small galaxy has been gliding past the Whirlpool for hundreds of millions of years.

As NGC 5195 drifts by, its gravitational muscle pumps up waves within the Whirlpool's pancake-shaped disk. The waves are like ripples in a pond generated when a rock is thrown in the water. When the waves pass through orbiting gas clouds within the disk, they squeeze the gaseous material along each arm's inner edge. The dark dusty material looks like gathering storm clouds. These dense clouds collapse, creating a wake of star birth, as seen in the bright-pink star-forming regions. The largest stars eventually sweep away the dusty cocoons with a torrent of radiation, hurricane-like stellar winds, and shock waves from supernova blasts. Bright-blue star clusters emerge from the mayhem, illuminating the Whirlpool's arms like city streetlights.

The Whirlpool is one of astronomy's galactic darlings. Located 31 million light-years away in the constellation Canes Venatici (the Hunting Dogs), the Whirlpool's beautiful face-on view and closeness to Earth allow astronomers to study a classic spiral galaxy's structure and star-forming processes.

Imagination of Man

Printing Press ~ Johann Gutenberg
(1439)

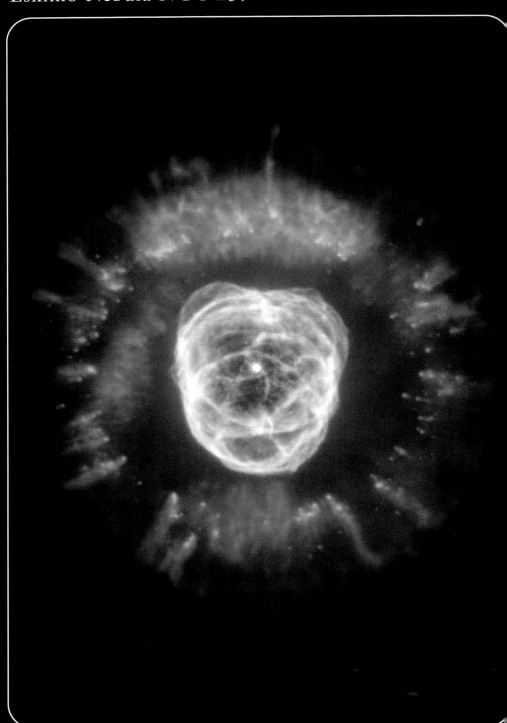

Eskimo Nebula NGC 2392

In its first glimpse of the heavens following the successful December 1999 servicing mission, NASA's Hubble Space Telescope has captured a majestic view of a planetary nebula, the glowing remains of a dying Sun-like star. This stellar relic, first spied by William Herschel in 1787, is nicknamed the "Eskimo" Nebula (NGC 2392) because, when viewed through ground-based telescopes, it resembles a face surrounded by a fur parka. In this Hubble Telescope image, the "parka" is really a disk of material embellished with a ring of comet-shaped objects with their tails streaming away from the central dying star. The Eskimo's "face" also contains some fascinating details. Although this bright central region resembles a ball of twine, it is, in reality, a bubble of material being blown into space by the central star's intense "wind" of high-speed material.

The planetary nebula began forming about 10,000 years ago, when the dying star began flinging material into space. The nebula is composed of two elliptically shaped lobes of matter streaming above and below the dying star. In this photo, one bubble lies in front of the other, obscuring part of the second lobe.

Scientists believe that a ring of dense material around the star's equator, ejected during its red giant phase, created the nebula's shape. This dense waist of material is plodding along at 72,000 miles per hour (115,000 kilometers per hour), preventing high-velocity stellar winds from pushing matter along the equator. Instead, the 900,000-mile-per-hour (1.5-million-kilometer-per-hour) winds are sweeping the material above and below the star, creating the elongated bubbles. The bubbles are not smooth like balloons but have filaments of denser matter. Each bubble is about one light-year long and about half a light-year wide. Scientists are still puzzled about the origin of the comet-shaped features in the "parka." One possible explanation is that these objects formed from a collision of slow- and fast-moving gases.

The Eskimo Nebula is about 5,000 light-years from Earth in the constellation Gemini. The picture was taken January 10 and 11, 2000, with the Wide Field and Planetary Camera 2. The nebula's glowing gases produce the colors in this image: nitrogen (red), hydrogen (green), oxygen (blue), and helium (violet).

Imagination of Man

Calculating Machines ~ Wilhelm Schickard
(1623)

Bubble Nebula NGC 7635

This NASA Hubble Space Telescope image reveals an expanding shell of glowing gas surrounding a hot massive star in our Milky Way galaxy. This shell is being shaped by strong stellar winds of material and radiation produced by the bright star at the left, which is ten to twenty times more massive than our Sun. These fierce winds are sculpting the surrounding material—composed of gas and dust—into the curve-shaped bubble.

Astronomers have dubbed it the Bubble Nebula NGC 7635. The nebula is ten light-years across, more than twice the distance from Earth to the nearest star. Only part of the bubble is visible in this image. The glowing gas in the lower right-hand corner is a dense region of material that is getting blasted by radiation from the Bubble Nebula's massive star. The radiation is eating into the gas, creating finger-like features. This interaction also heats up the gas, causing it to glow.

The remarkably spherical "bubble" marks the boundary between an intense wind of particles from the star and the more quiescent interior of the nebula. The central star of the nebula is forty times more massive than the Sun and is responsible for a stellar wind moving at 2,000 kilometers per second (four million miles per hour or seven million kilometers per hour) which propels particles off the surface of the star. The bubble surface actually marks the leading edge of this wind's gust front, which is slowing as it plows into the denser surrounding material.

The surface of the bubble is not uniform because as the shell expands outward it encounters regions of the cold gas, which are of different density and therefore arrest the expansion by differing amounts, resulting in the rippled appearance. It is this gradient of background material that the wind is encountering that places the central star off-center in the bubble. There is more material to the northeast of the nebula than to the southwest, so that the wind progresses less in that direction, offsetting the central star from the geometric center of the bubble. At a distance of 7,100 light-years from Earth, the Bubble Nebula is located in the constellation Cassiopeia and has a diameter of six light-years.

Imagination of Man

Dishwasher ~ Josephine Cochran
(1886)

Elephant's Trunk Nebula

NASA's Spitzer Space Telescope has captured a glowing stellar nursery within a dark globule that is opaque at visible light. These new images pierce through the obscuration to reveal the birth of new protostars, or embryonic stars, and young stars never before seen. The Elephant's Trunk Nebula is an elongated dark globule within the emission nebula IC 1396 in the constellation of Cepheus. Located at a distance of 2,450 light-years, the globule is a condensation of dense gas that is barely surviving the strong ionizing radiation from a nearby massive star. The globule is being compressed by the surrounding ionized gas.

The large composite image on the left is a product of combining data from the observatory's multiband imaging photometer and the infrared array camera. The thermal emission at 24 microns measured by the photometer (red) is combined with near-infrared emission from the camera at 3.6/4.5 microns (blue) and from 5.8/8.0 microns (green). The colors of the diffuse emission and filaments vary, and are a combination of molecular hydrogen (which tends to be green) and polycyclic aromatic hydrocarbon (brown) emissions.

Within the globule, a half dozen newly discovered protostars are easily discernible as the bright-red tinted objects, mostly along the southern rim of the globule. These were previously undetected at visible wavelengths due to obscuration by the thick cloud ("globule body") and by dust surrounding the newly forming stars. The newborn stars form in the dense gas because of compression by the wind and radiation from a nearby massive star (located outside the field of view to the left). The winds from this unseen star are also responsible for producing the spectacular filamentary appearance of the globule itself, which resembles that of a flying dragon.

The Spitzer Space Telescope also sees many newly discovered young stars, often enshrouded in dust, which may be starting the nuclear fusion that defines a star. These young stars are too cool to be seen at visible wavelengths. Both the protostars and young stars are bright in the mid-infrared because of their surrounding discs of solid material. A few of the visible light stars in this image were found to have excess infrared emission, suggesting they are more mature stars surrounded by primordial remnants from their formation, or from crumbling asteroids and comets in their planetary systems.

Imagination of Man

The Phonograph ~ Thomas Edison
(1877)

153

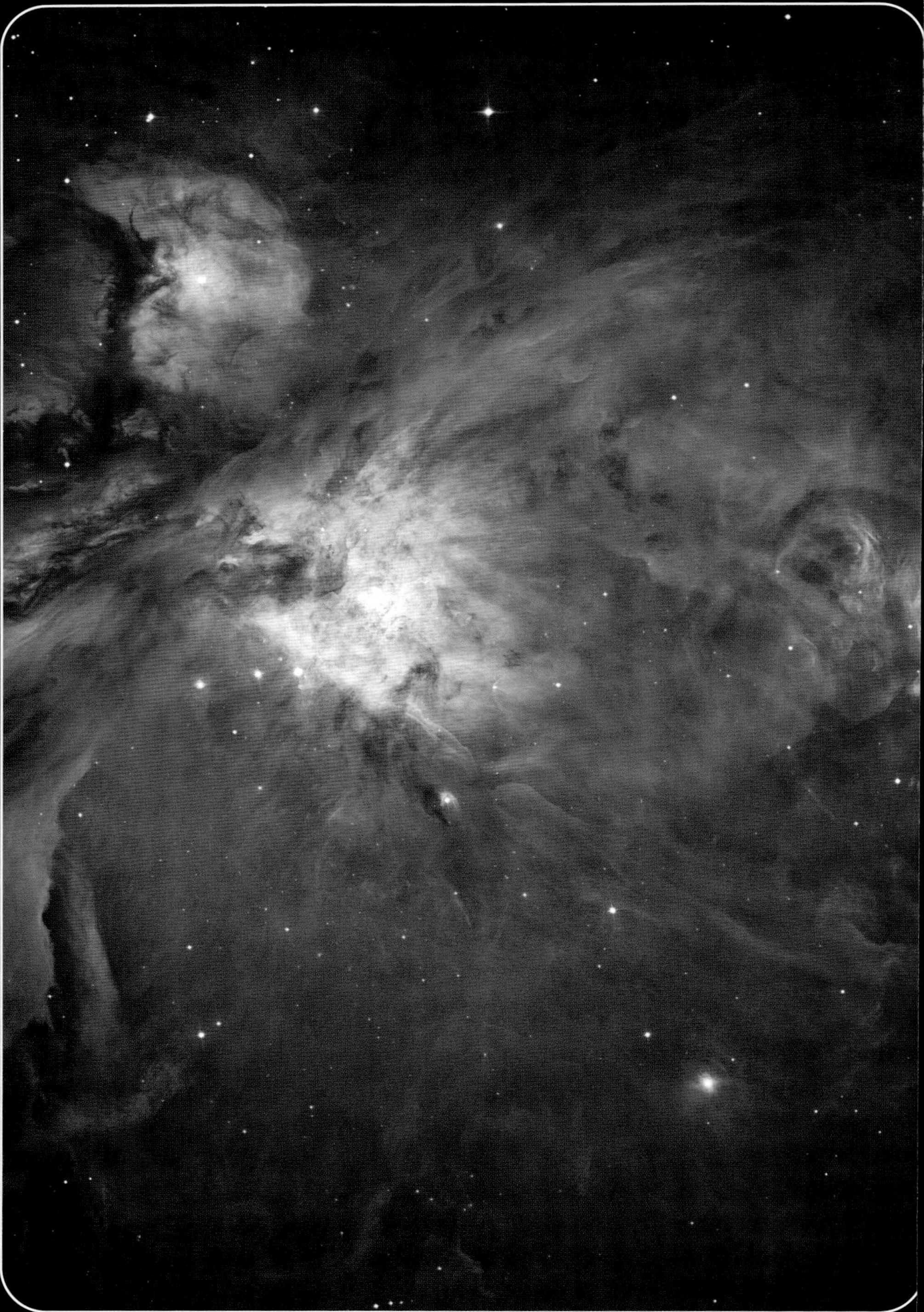

Orion Nebula M42, NGC 1976

This dramatic image offers a peek inside a cavern of roiling dust and gas where thousands of stars are forming. The image, taken by the Advanced Camera for Surveys (ACS) aboard NASA's Hubble Space Telescope, represents the sharpest view ever taken of this region, called the Orion Nebula. More than 3,000 stars of various sizes appear in this image. Some of them have never been seen in visible light. These stars reside in a dramatic dust-and-gas landscape of plateaus, mountains, and valleys that are reminiscent of the Grand Canyon.

The Orion Nebula is a picture book of star formation, from the massive young stars that are shaping the nebula to the pillars of dense gas that may be the homes of budding stars. The bright central region is the home of the four heftiest stars in the nebula. The stars are called the Trapezium because they are arranged in a trapezoid pattern. Ultraviolet light unleashed by these stars is carving a cavity in the nebula and disrupting the growth of hundreds of smaller stars. Located near the Trapezium stars are stars still young enough to have disks of material encircling them. These disks are called protoplanetary disks or "proplyds" and are too small to see clearly in this image. The disks are the building blocks of solar systems.

The bright glow at the upper left is from M43, a small region being shaped by a massive young star's ultraviolet light. Astronomers call the region a miniature Orion Nebula because only one star is sculpting the landscape. The Orion Nebula has four such stars. Next to M43 are dense dark pillars of dust and gas that point toward the Trapezium. These pillars are resisting erosion from the Trapezium's intense ultraviolet light. The glowing region on the right reveals arcs and bubbles formed when stellar winds—streams of charged particles ejected from the Trapezium stars—collide with material.

The faint-red stars near the bottom are the myriad brown dwarfs that Hubble spied for the first time in the nebula in visible light. Sometimes called "failed stars," brown dwarfs are cool objects that are too small to be ordinary stars because they cannot sustain nuclear fusion in their cores the way our Sun does. The dark-red column, below left, shows an illuminated edge of the cavity wall. The Orion Nebula is 1,500 light-years away, the nearest star-forming region to Earth.

Imagination of Man

The *Mona Lisa* ~ Leonardo da Vinci
(1519)

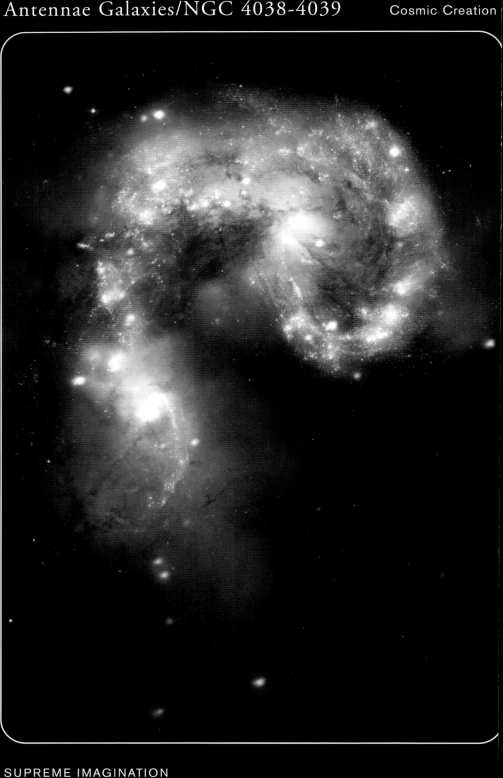

Antennae Galaxies NGC 4038-4039

A new image of two tangled galaxies has been released by NASA's Great Observatories. The Antennae galaxies, located about 62 million light-years from Earth, are shown in this composite image from the Chandra X-ray Observatory (blue), the Hubble Space Telescope (gold and brown), and the Spitzer Space Telescope (red). The Antennae galaxies take their name from the long, antenna-like arms seen in wide-angle views of the system. These features were produced in the collision.

The collision, which began more than 100 million years ago and is still occurring, has triggered the formation of millions of stars in clouds of dusts and gas in the galaxies. The most massive of these young stars have already sped through their evolution in a few million years and exploded as supernovas.

The X-ray image from Chandra shows huge clouds of hot, interstellar gas, which have been injected with rich deposits of elements from supernova explosions. This enriched gas, which includes elements such as oxygen, iron, magnesium and silicon, will be incorporated into new generations of stars and planets. The bright, point-like sources in the image are produced by material falling onto black holes and neutron stars that are remnants of the massive stars. Some of these black holes may have masses that are almost one hundred times that of the sun.

The Spitzer data show infrared light from warm dust clouds that have been heated by newborn stars, with the brightest clouds lying in the overlap region between the two galaxies. The Hubble data reveal old stars and star-forming regions in gold and white, while filaments of dust appear in brown. Many of the fainter objects in the optical image are clusters containing thousands of stars.

Imagination of Man

Sundial ~ Anaximander
(611-547)

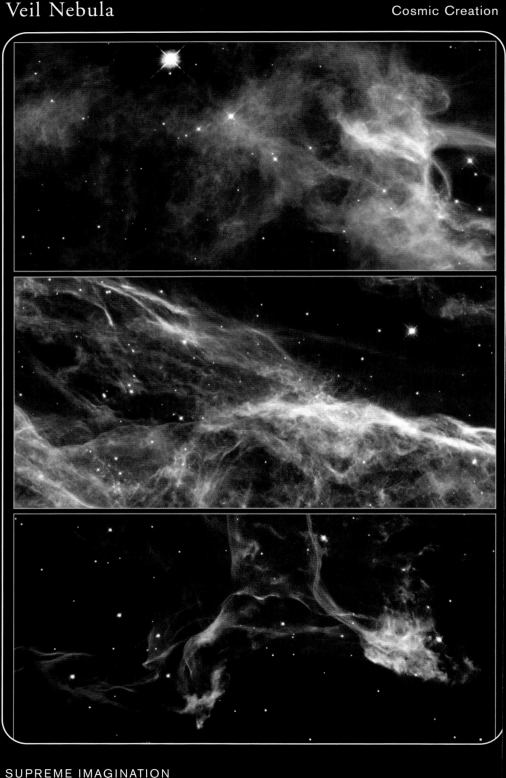

Veil Nebula

NASA's Hubble Space Telescope photographed three magnificent sections of the Veil Nebula—the shattered remains of a supernova that exploded thousands of years ago. This series of images provides beautifully detailed views of the delicate, wispy structure resulting from this cosmic explosion. The Veil Nebula is one of the most spectacular supernova remnants. The entire shell spans three degrees on the sky, about six full moons.

The Veil Nebula is a prototypical middle-aged supernova remnant, and is an ideal laboratory for studying the physics of supernova remnants because of its unobscured location in our galaxy, its relative closeness, and its large size. Also known as the Cygnus Loop, the Veil Nebula is located in the constellation of Cygnus, the Swan. It is 1,500 light-years away from Earth.

Stars in our galaxy and others are born and then die. How long a star lives depends on how massive it is. The more massive the star, the shorter its life. When a star significantly larger than our Sun runs out of fuel, it collapses and blows itself apart in a catastrophic supernova explosion. A supernova releases so much light that it can outshine a whole galaxy of stars put together. The exploding star sweeps out a huge bubble in its surroundings, fringed with actual stellar debris along with material swept up by the blast wave. This glowing, brightly colored shell of gas forms a nebula that astronomers call a "supernova remnant." Such a remnant can remain visible long after the initial explosion fades away. Scientists estimate that the Veil supernova explosion occurred some 5,000 to 10,000 years ago.

The small regions captured in these Hubble images provide stunning close-ups of the Veil. Fascinating smoke-like wisps of gas are all that remain visible of what was once a star in our Milky Way galaxy. The intertwined rope-like filaments of gas in the Veil Nebula result from the enormous amounts of energy released as the fast-moving debris from the explosion plows into its surroundings and creates shock fronts. These shocks, driven by debris moving at 600,000 kilometers per hour, heat the gas to millions of degrees. It is the subsequent cooling of this material that produces brilliant glowing colors.

Although only about one star per century in our galaxy will end its life in this spectacular way, these explosions are responsible for making all chemical elements heavier than iron, as well as being the main producers of oxygen in the Universe. Elements such as copper, mercury, gold, and lead are forged in these violent events. The expanding shells of supernova remnants mix with other clouds in the Milky Way and become the raw material for new generations of stars and planets. The chemical elements that constitute Earth, and indeed those of which we ourselves are made, were formed deep inside ancient stars and distributed by supernova explosions in nebulae like the one we see here.

Imagination of Man

Romeo and Juliet ~ William Shakespeare (1591-1595)

Barred Spiral Galaxy NGC 1300

One of the largest Hubble Space Telescope images ever made of a complete galaxy has just been unveiled at the American Astronomical Society meeting in San Diego, California. The Hubble Telescope captured a display of starlight, glowing gas, and silhouetted dark clouds of interstellar dust in this four-foot by eight-foot image of the Barred Spiral Galaxy NGC 1300. NGC 1300 is considered to be prototypical of barred spiral galaxies. Barred spirals differ from normal spiral galaxies in that the arms of the galaxy do not spiral all the way into the center, but are connected to the two ends of a straight bar of stars containing the nucleus at its center.

At Hubble's resolution, a myriad of fine details, some of which have never before been seen, can be glimpsed throughout the galaxy's arms, disk, bulge, and nucleus. Blue and red supergiant stars, star clusters, and star-forming regions are well resolved across the spiral arms, and dust lanes trace out fine structures in the disk and bar. Numerous more distant galaxies are visible in the background, and are seen even through the densest regions of NGC 1300.

In the core of the larger spiral structure of NGC 1300, the nucleus shows its own extraordinary and distinct "grand-design" spiral structure that is about 3,300 light-years (1 kiloparsec) long. Only galaxies with large-scale bars appear to have these grand-design inner disks—a spiral within a spiral. Models suggest that the gas in a bar can be funneled inward, and then spiral into the center through the grand-design disk, where it can potentially fuel a central black hole. NGC 1300 is not known to have an active nucleus, however, indicating either that there is no black hole or that it is not accreting matter.

The image was constructed from exposures taken in September 2004 by the Advanced Camera for Surveys onboard Hubble in four filters. Starlight and dust are seen in blue, visible, and infrared light. Bright star clusters are highlighted in red by their associated emission from glowing hydrogen gas. Due to the galaxy's large size, two adjacent pointings of the telescope were necessary to cover the extent of the spiral arms. The galaxy lies roughly sixty-nine million light-years away (twenty-one megaparsecs) in the direction of the constellation Eridanus.

Imagination of Man

Double-Action Pedal Harp ~ Sebastian Erard
(1801)

SUPREME IMAGINATION

Pleiades Star Cluster M45

The brilliant stars seen in this image are members of the popular open-star cluster known as the Pleiades, or Seven Sisters. About 1,000 stars comprise the cluster, located in the constellation Taurus.

Astronomers using NASA's Hubble Space Telescope have helped settle a mystery that has puzzled scientists concerning the exact distance to the famous nearby star cluster known as the Pleiades, or the Seven Sisters. The Pleiades cluster, named by the ancient Greeks, is easily seen as a small grouping of stars lying near the shoulder of Taurus, the Bull, in the winter sky. Although it might be expected that the distance to this well-studied cluster would be well established, there has been an ongoing controversy among astronomers about its distance for the past seven years.

The mystery began in 1997, when the European Space Agency's satellite, Hipparcos, measured the distance to the Pleiades and found it was ten percent closer to Earth than traditional estimates, which had been based on comparing the Pleiades to nearby stars. If the Hipparcos measurements were correct, then the stars in the Pleiades are peculiar because they are fainter than Sun-like stars would be at that distance. This finding, if substantiated, would challenge our basic understanding of the structure of stars.

But measurements made by the Hubble telescope's "fine guidance sensors" showed that the distance to the Pleiades is about 440 light-years from Earth, essentially the same as past distance estimates and differing from the Hipparcos results by more than forty light-years. The new results agree with recent measurements made by astronomers at the California Institute of Technology and NASA's Jet Propulsion Laboratory, both in Pasadena, California. Those astronomers used interferometer measurements from Mt. Wilson and Palomar observatories in California, which found that the star cluster is between 434 and 446 light-years from Earth.

The color-composite image of the Pleiades star cluster was taken by the Palomar's 48-inch Schmidt telescope. The image is from the second Palomar Observatory Sky Survey, and is part of the Digitized Sky Survey. The Pleiades photo was made from three separate images taken in red, green, and blue filters. The separate images were taken between November 5, 1986, and September 11, 1996.

Imagination of Man

Electric Guitar ~ A. de Torres
(1931)

Reflection Nebula NGC 7129

Out of the dark and dusty cosmos comes an unusual Valentine—a stellar nursery resembling a shimmering pink rosebud. This cluster of newborn stars, called a "reflection nebula," was captured by state-of-the-art infrared detectors onboard NASA's new Spitzer Space Telescope, formerly known as the Space Infrared Telescope Facility.

"The picture is more than just pretty," said the principal investigator for the latest observations and an astronomer at the Harvard Smithsonian Center for Astrophysics in Cambridge, Massachusetts. "It helps us understand how stars form in the crowded environments of stellar nurseries."

Located 3,330 light-years away in the constellation Cepheus and spanning ten light-years across, the rosebud-shaped nebula, numbered NGC 7129, is home to some 130 young stars. Our own Sun is believed to have grown up in a similar family setting.

Previous images of NGC 7129 taken by visible telescopes show a smattering of hazy stars spotted against a luminescent cloud. Spitzer, by sensing the infrared radiation or heat of the cluster, produces a much more detailed snapshot. Highlighted in false colors are the hot dust particles and gases, respectively, which form a nest around the stars. The pink rosebud contains adolescent stars that blew away blankets of hot dust, while the green stem holds newborn stars whose jets torched surrounding gases.

Outside of the primary nebula, younger proto-stars can also be seen for the first time. "We can now see a few stars beyond the nebula that were previously hidden in the dark cloud."

In addition, the findings go beyond what can be seen in the image. By analyzing the amount and type of infrared light emitted by nearly every star in the cluster, scientists were able to determine which ones support the swirling rings of debris, called "circumstellar disks," which eventually coalesce to form planets. Roughly half of the stars observed were found to harbor disks.

These observations will ultimately help astronomers determine how stellar nurseries shape the development of planetary systems similar to our own.

Imagination of Man

Liquid Fuel Rockets ~ Robert Goddard
(1926)

Moon's View From Columbia

From time to time men and women risk their lives for what they love and believe in. They have such a passion for what they do it is as if they are pulled by some uncontrollable magnetic force that draws them in. Many times, even if they make attempts to escape it, the attraction is too strong and too irresistible. Through their imagination they can see what others cannot envision. It is that small voice within them that keeps pushing them, whispering: "You can do it, don't give up, ignore what they are saying, take the risk, just go for it." When things go wrong, and they do, we can't fault them, because they were compelled beyond their ability to turn back.

In their quest to explore and understand the Universe, the crew members of the Space Shuttle Columbia lost their lives after they recorded this digital photo of the moon on their final mission. On February 1, 2003, the shuttle broke up on re-entry into the Earth's atmosphere. Perhaps, as they looked upon this awe-inspiring view of the moon for the final time they felt a sense of awe toward the one whose imagination was responsible for this inspiring view.

Their love for space exploration and their quest to respond to the invitation uttered so long ago *"Look up into the heavens. Who created all the stars?"* ultimately cost them their lives, but their lives were not lost in vain. It is through the tireless dedication of them and others like them that we have been given this glimpse into the mind of Imagination Supreme. Without their efforts, this wonderful Gallery of Cosmic Creations to inspire us and build our appreciation for the heavens above, and their Designer would not be possible. It is through their dedication and pioneering of space that we now have a front row seat of the Grandest Drama to ever unfold before human eyes!

Imagination of Man

Space Shuttle ~ NASA
(1981)

Reflection Nebula NGC 1999

Just weeks after NASA astronauts repaired the Hubble Space Telescope in December 1999, the Hubble Heritage Project snapped this picture of NGC 1999, a nebula in the constellation Orion. NGC 1999 is an example of a reflection nebula. Like fog around a street lamp, a reflection nebula shines only because the light from an embedded source illuminates its dust; the nebula does not emit any visible light of its own. NGC 1999 lies close to the famous Orion Nebula, about 1,500 light-years from Earth, in a region of our Milky Way galaxy where new stars are being formed actively. The nebula is famous in astronomical history because the first Herbig-Haro object was discovered immediately adjacent to it (it lies just outside the new Hubble image). Herbig-Haro objects are now known to be jets of gas ejected from very young stars.

The NGC 1999 nebula is illuminated by a bright, recently formed star, visible in the Hubble photo just to the left of center. This star is cataloged as V380 Orionis, and its white color is due to its high surface temperature of about 10,000 degrees Celsius (nearly twice that of our own Sun). Its mass is estimated to be 3.5 times that of the Sun. The star is so young that it is still surrounded by a cloud of material left over from its formation, here seen as the NGC 1999 reflection nebula.

The WFPC2 image of NGC 1999 shows a remarkable jet-black cloud near its center, resembling the letter "T" tilted on its side, located just to the right and lower right of the bright star. This dark cloud is an example of a "Bok globule," named after the late University of Arizona astronomer Bart Bok. The globule is a cold cloud of gas, molecules, and cosmic dust, which is so dense it blocks all of the light behind it. In the Hubble image, the globule is seen silhouetted against the reflection nebula illuminated by V380 Orionis. Astronomers believe that new stars may be forming inside Bok globules through the contraction of the dust and molecular gas under their own gravity.

NGC 1999 was discovered some two centuries ago by Sir William Herschel and his sister Caroline, and was catalogued later in the nineteenth century as object 1999 in the New General Catalogue.

Imagination of Man

Airplane ~ Orville & Wilbur Wright
(1903)

Black Eye Galaxy M64

A collision of two galaxies has left a merged star system with an unusual appearance as well as bizarre internal motions. Messier 64 (M64) has a spectacular dark band of absorbing dust in front of the galaxy's bright nucleus, giving rise to its nicknames of the "Black Eye" or "Evil Eye" galaxy.

Fine details of the dark band are revealed in this image of the central portion of M64 obtained with the Hubble Space Telescope. M64 is well known among amateur astronomers because of its appearance in small telescopes. It was first catalogued in the eighteenth century by the French astronomer Messier. Located in the northern constellation Coma Berenices, M64 resides roughly seventeen million light-years from Earth.

At first glance, M64 appears to be a fairly normal pinwheel-shaped spiral galaxy. As in the majority of galaxies, all of the stars in M64 are rotating in the same direction, clockwise, as seen in the Hubble image. However, detailed studies in the 1990s led to the remarkable discovery that the interstellar gas in the outer regions of M64 rotates in the opposite direction from the gas and stars in the inner regions.

Active formation of new stars is occurring in the shear region where the contrarily rotating gases collide, are compressed, and contract. Particularly noticeable in the image are hot, blue, young stars that have just formed, along with pink clouds of glowing hydrogen gas that fluoresce when exposed to ultraviolet light from newly formed stars.

Astronomers believe that the oppositely rotating gas arose when M64 absorbed a satellite galaxy that collided with it, perhaps more than one billion years ago. This small galaxy has now been almost completely destroyed, but signs of the collision persist in the backward motion of gas at the outer edge of M64.

Imagination of Man

Communication Satellites ~ Soviet Union
(1957)

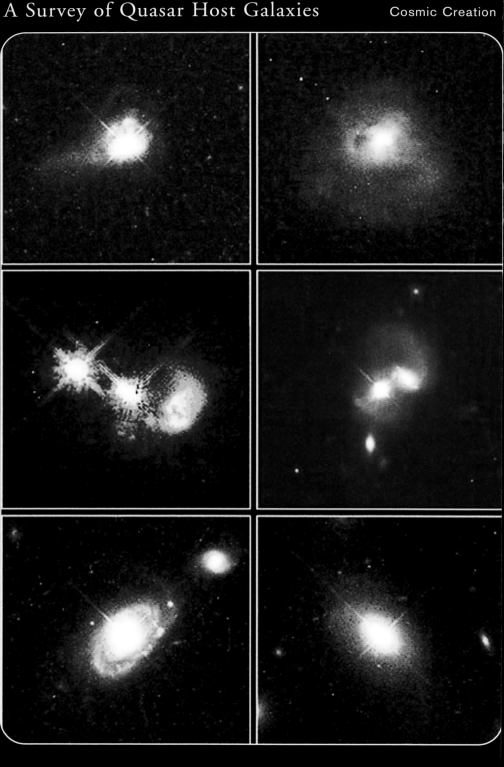

A Survey of Quasar Host Galaxies

Quasars reside in a variety of galaxies, from normal to highly disturbed. When seen through ground-based telescopes, these compact enigmatic light sources resemble stars, yet they are billions of light-years away and several hundred billion times brighter than normal stars. The following Hubble Space Telescope images show examples of different home sites of all quasars. But all the sites must provide the fuel to power these unique light beacons. Astronomers believe that a quasar turns on when a massive black hole at the nucleus of a galaxy feeds on gas and stars. As the matter falls into the black hole, intense radiation is emitted. Eventually, the black hole will stop emitting radiation once it consumes all nearby matter. Then it needs debris from a collision of galaxies or another process to provide more fuel. The column of images on the left represents normal galaxies; the center, colliding galaxies; and the right, peculiar galaxies.

Two teams of astronomers are releasing dramatic Hubble Space Telescope images soon, which show that quasars live in a remarkable variety of galaxies, many of which are violently colliding. This complicated picture suggests there may be a variety of mechanisms—some quite subtle—for "turning on" quasars, the universe's most energetic objects.

The Hubble researchers are also intrigued by the fact that the quasars studied do not appear to have obviously damaged the galaxies in which they live. This could mean that quasars are relatively short-lived phenomena which many galaxies, including the Milky Way, experienced long ago.

Discovered only thirty-three years ago, quasars are among the most baffling objects in the universe because of their small size and prodigious energy output. Quasars are not much bigger than Earth's solar system but pour out 100 to 1,000 times as much light as an entire galaxy containing a hundred billion stars.

A super-massive black hole, gobbling up stars, gas, and dust, is theorized to be the "engine" powering a quasar. Most astronomers agree an active black hole is the only credible explanation as to how quasars can be so compact, variable, and powerful. Nevertheless, conclusive evidence has been elusive because quasars are so bright they mask any details of the "environment" where they live.

The luminosity of quasars, therefore, is thought to be about two to ten trillion times that of our Sun, or about 100 to 1,000 times that of the total light of average giant galaxies like our Milky Way.

Imagination of Man

Telescope ~ Hans Lippershy
(1608)

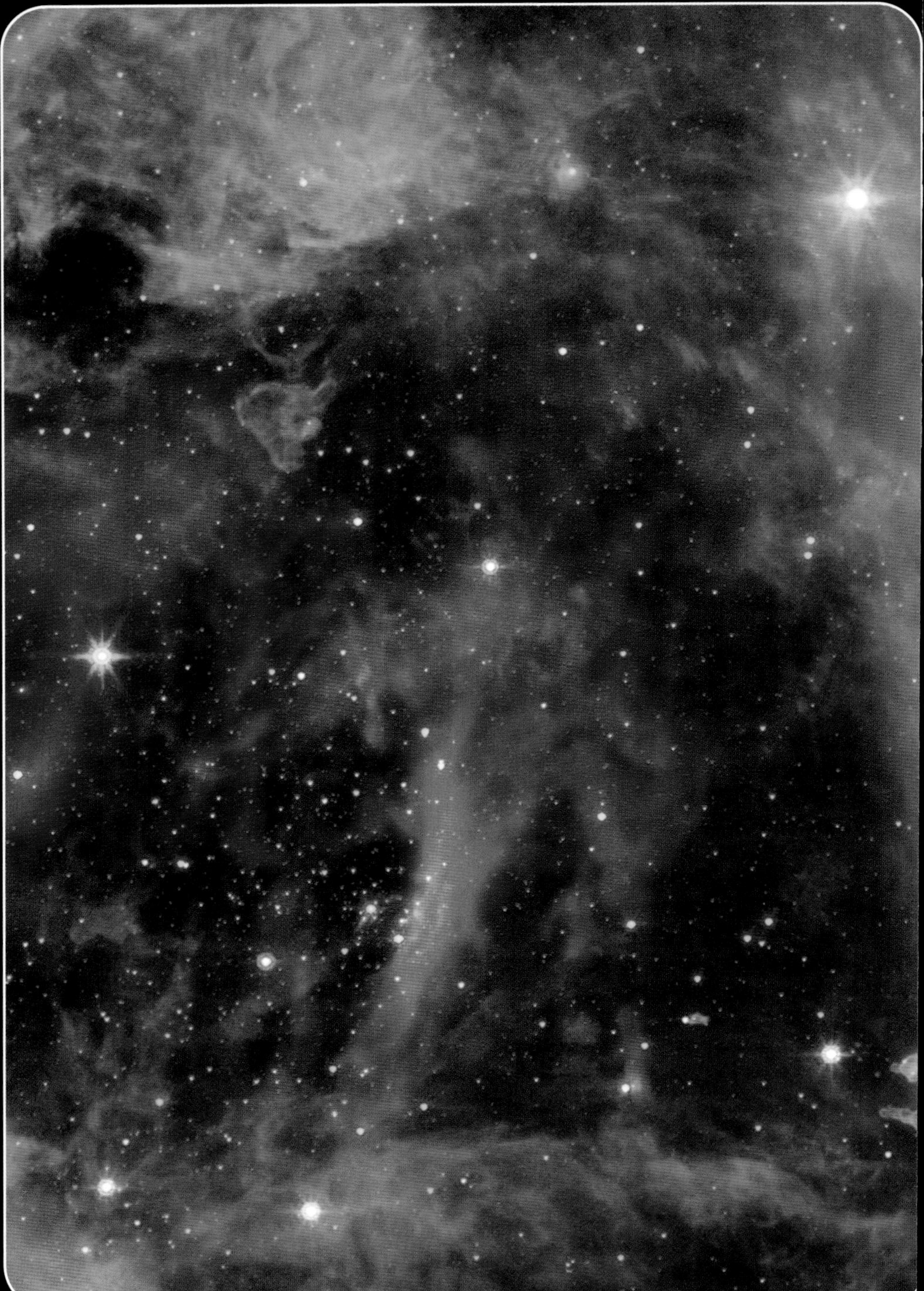

Star-Forming Rosette Nebula NGC 2244

This infrared image from NASA's Spitzer Space Telescope shows the Rosette nebula, a pretty star-forming region more than 5,000 light-years away in the constellation Monoceros. In optical light, the nebula looks like a rosebud, or the "rosette" adornments that date back to antiquity. But lurking inside this delicate cosmic rosebud are super-hot stars called O-stars, whose radiation and winds have collectively excavated layers of dust (green) and gas away, revealing the cavity of cooler dust (red). Some of the Rosette's O-stars can be seen in the bubble-like red cavity; however, the largest two blue stars in this picture are in the foreground, and not in the nebula itself.

Astronomers have laid down the cosmic equivalent of yellow "caution" tape around super-hot stars, marking the zones where cooler stars are in danger of having their developing planets blasted away.

In a new study from NASA's Spitzer Space Telescope, scientists report the first maps of so-called planetary "danger zones." These are areas where winds and radiation from super-hot stars can strip other young, cooler stars like our Sun of their planet-forming materials. The results show that cooler stars are safe as long as they lie at least 1.6 light-years, or nearly ten trillion miles, from any hot stars. But cooler stars inside the zone are likely to see their potential planets boiled off into space.

The observations revealed that, beyond ten trillion miles of an O-star, about 45 percent of the stars had disks—about the same amount as there were in safer neighborhoods free of O-stars. Within this distance, only 27 percent of the stars had disks, with fewer and fewer disks spotted around stars closest to the O-star. In other words, an O-star's danger zone is a sphere whose damaging effects are worst at the core. For reference, our Sun's closest star, a small star called Proxima Centauri, is nearly thirty trillion miles away.

Some astronomers think our Sun was born in a similarly violent neighborhood studded with O-stars before migrating to its present, more spacious home. If so, it was lucky enough to escape a harrowing ride into any danger zones, otherwise our planets and life as we know it would not be here today.

Imagination of Man

Wireless Communication ~ Guglielmo Marconi
(1895)

Earth

Earth, our home planet, is the only planet in our solar system known to harbor life —life that is incredibly diverse. All of the things we need to survive are provided under a thin layer of atmosphere that separates us from the uninhabitable void of space. Earth is made up of complex interactive systems that are often unpredictable. Air, water, land, and life—including humans—combine forces to create a constantly changing world that we are striving to understand.

Viewing Earth from the unique perspective of space provides the opportunity to see Earth as a whole. Scientists around the world have discovered many things about our planet by working together and sharing their findings. Some facts are well known. For instance, Earth is the third planet from the Sun and the fifth largest in the solar system. Earth's diameter is just a few hundred kilometers larger than that of Venus's. The four seasons are a result of Earth's axis of rotation being tilted more than 23 degrees.

Oceans at least four kilometers deep cover nearly 70 percent of the Earth's surface. Fresh water exists in the liquid phase only within a narrow temperature span (0 degrees to 100 degrees Celsius). This temperature span is especially narrow when contrasted with the full range of temperatures found within the solar system. The presence and distribution of water vapor in the atmosphere is responsible for much of Earth's weather. Near the surface, an ocean of air that consists of 78 percent nitrogen, 21 percent oxygen, and 1 percent other ingredients envelops us. This atmosphere affects Earth's long-term climate and short-term local weather; shields us from nearly all harmful radiation coming from the Sun; and protects us from meteors as well—most of which burn up before they can strike the surface. Satellites have revealed that the upper atmosphere actually swells by day and contracts by night due to solar activity.

Our planet's rapid spin and molten nickel-iron core give rise to a magnetic field, which the solar wind distorts into a teardrop shape. The solar wind is a stream of charged particles continuously ejected from the Sun.

Imagination of Man

Spitzer Space Telescope ~ NASA
(2003)

Cone Nebula NGC 2264

Resembling a nightmarish beast rearing its head from a crimson sea, this monstrous object is actually an innocuous pillar of gas and dust. Called the Cone Nebula NGC 2264—so named because, in ground-based images, it has a conical shape—this giant pillar resides in a turbulent star-forming region.

This picture taken by the newly installed Advanced Camera for Surveys (ACS) aboard NASA's Hubble Space Telescope shows the upper 2.5 light-years of the nebula, a height that equals twenty-three million round trips to the Moon. The entire nebula is seven light-years long. The Cone Nebula resides 2,500 light-years away in the constellation Monoceros.

Radiation from hot young stars (located beyond the top of the image) has slowly eroded the nebula over millions of years. Ultraviolet light heats the edges of the dark cloud, releasing gas into the relatively empty region of surrounding space. There, additional ultraviolet radiation causes the hydrogen gas to glow, which produces the red halo of light seen around the pillar. A similar process occurs on a much smaller scale to gas surrounding a single star, forming the bow-shaped arc seen near the upper left side of the Cone. This arc, seen previously with the Hubble Telescope, is sixty-five times larger than the diameter of our solar system. The blue-white light from surrounding stars is reflected by dust. Background stars can be seen peeking through the evaporating tendrils of gas, while the turbulent base is pockmarked with stars reddened by dust.

Over time, only the densest regions of the Cone will be left. Inside these regions, stars and planets may form. The Cone Nebula is a cousin of the M16 pillars, which the Hubble Telescope imaged in 1995. Monstrous pillars of cold gas, like the Cone and M16, are common in large regions of star birth. Astronomers believe that these pillars are incubators for developing stars.

Imagination of Man

Geobond ~ Patricia Billings
(1997)

Mars

The red planet Mars has inspired wild flights of imagination over the centuries, as well as intense scientific interest. Whether fancied to be the source of hostile invaders of Earth, the home of a dying civilization, or a rough-and-tumble mining colony of the future, Mars provides fertile ground for science fiction writers, based on seeds planted by centuries of scientific observations.

We know that Mars is a small rocky body once thought to be very Earth-like. Like the other "terrestrial" planets—Mercury, Venus, and Earth—its surface has been changed by volcanism, impacts from other bodies, movements of its crust, and atmospheric effects such as dust storms. It has polar ice caps that grow and recede with the change of seasons; areas of layered soils near the Martian poles suggest that the planet's climate has changed more than once, perhaps caused by a regular change in the planet's orbit. Martian tectonism—the formation and change of a planet's crust—differs from Earth's. Where Earth tectonics involve sliding plates that grind against each other or spread apart in the seafloors, Martian tectonics seem to be vertical with hot lava pushing upward through the crust to the surface. Periodically, great dust storms engulf the entire planet. The effects of these storms are dramatic, including giant dunes, wind streaks, and wind-carved features.

Scientists believe that 3.5 billion years ago, Mars experienced the largest known floods in the solar system. This water may even have pooled into lakes or shallow oceans. But where did the ancient flood water come from, how long did it last, and where did it go? In May 2002, scientists announced the discovery of a key piece in the puzzle: the Mars Odyssey spacecraft had detected large quantities of water ice close to the surface—enough to fill Lake Michigan twice over. The ice is mixed into the soil only a meter (about three feet) below the surface of a wide area near the Martian south pole.

Many questions remain. At present, Mars is too cold and its atmosphere is too thin to allow liquid water to exist at the surface for long. More water exists frozen in the polar ice caps, and enough water exists to form ice clouds, but the quantity of water required to carve Mars' great channels and flood plains is not evident on—or near—the surface today. Images from NASA's Mars Global Surveyor spacecraft suggest that underground reserves of water may break through the surface as springs. The answers may lie deep beneath Mars' red soil.

Imagination of Man

Interplanetary Spacecraft ~ NASA
(1962)

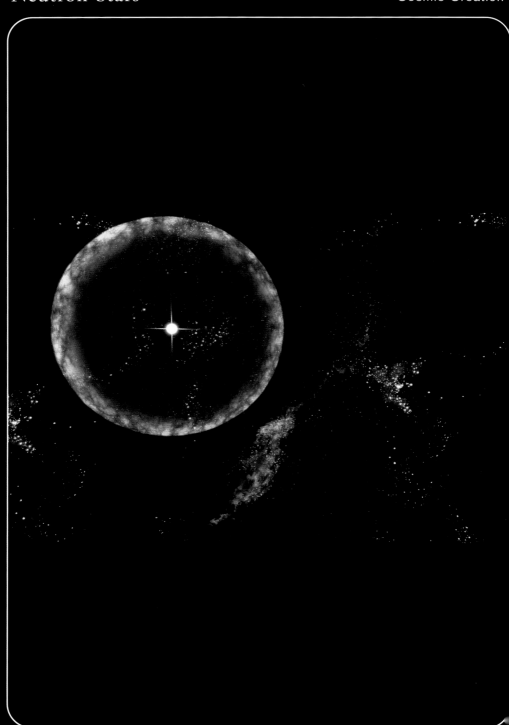

Neutron Stars

Scientists have detected a flash of light from across the Galaxy so powerful that it bounced off the Moon and lit up the Earth's upper atmosphere. The flash was brighter than anything ever detected from beyond our solar system and lasted over a tenth of a second. NASA and European satellites and many radio telescopes detected the flash and its aftermath on December 27, 2004.

The scientists said, as depicted in this artist's concept, that the light came from a "giant flare" on the surface of an exotic neutron star, called a magnetar. The apparent magnitude was brighter than a full moon and all historical star explosions. The light was brightest in the Gamma-ray energy range, far more energetic than visible light or X-rays and invisible to our eyes.

A neutron star is about twenty kilometers in diameter and has the mass of about 1.4 times that of our Sun. This means that a neutron star is so dense that on Earth, one teaspoonful would weigh a billion tons! Because of its small size and high density, a neutron star possesses a surface gravitational field about 2×10^{11} times that of Earth. Neutron stars can also have magnetic fields a million times stronger than the strongest magnetic fields produced on Earth.

Neutron stars are one of the possible ends for a star. They result from massive stars which have mass greater than four to eight times that of our Sun. After these stars have finished burning their nuclear fuel, they undergo a supernova explosion. This explosion blows off the outer layers of a star into a beautiful supernova remnant. The central region of the star collapses under gravity. It collapses so much that protons and electrons combine to form neutrons. Hence the name "neutron star."

Neutron stars may appear in supernova remnants, as isolated objects, or in binary systems. Four neutron stars are thought to have planets. When a neutron star is in a binary system, astronomers are able to measure its mass. From a number of such binaries seen with radio or X-ray telescopes, neutron-star masses have been found to be about 1.4 times the mass of the Sun. For binary systems containing an unknown object, this information helps distinguish whether the object is a neutron star or a black hole, since black holes are more massive than neutron stars.

Imagination of Man

Internal Combustion Engine ~ François Isaac de Rivaz
(1806)

Gas Plume Near the Edge of the Orion Nebula

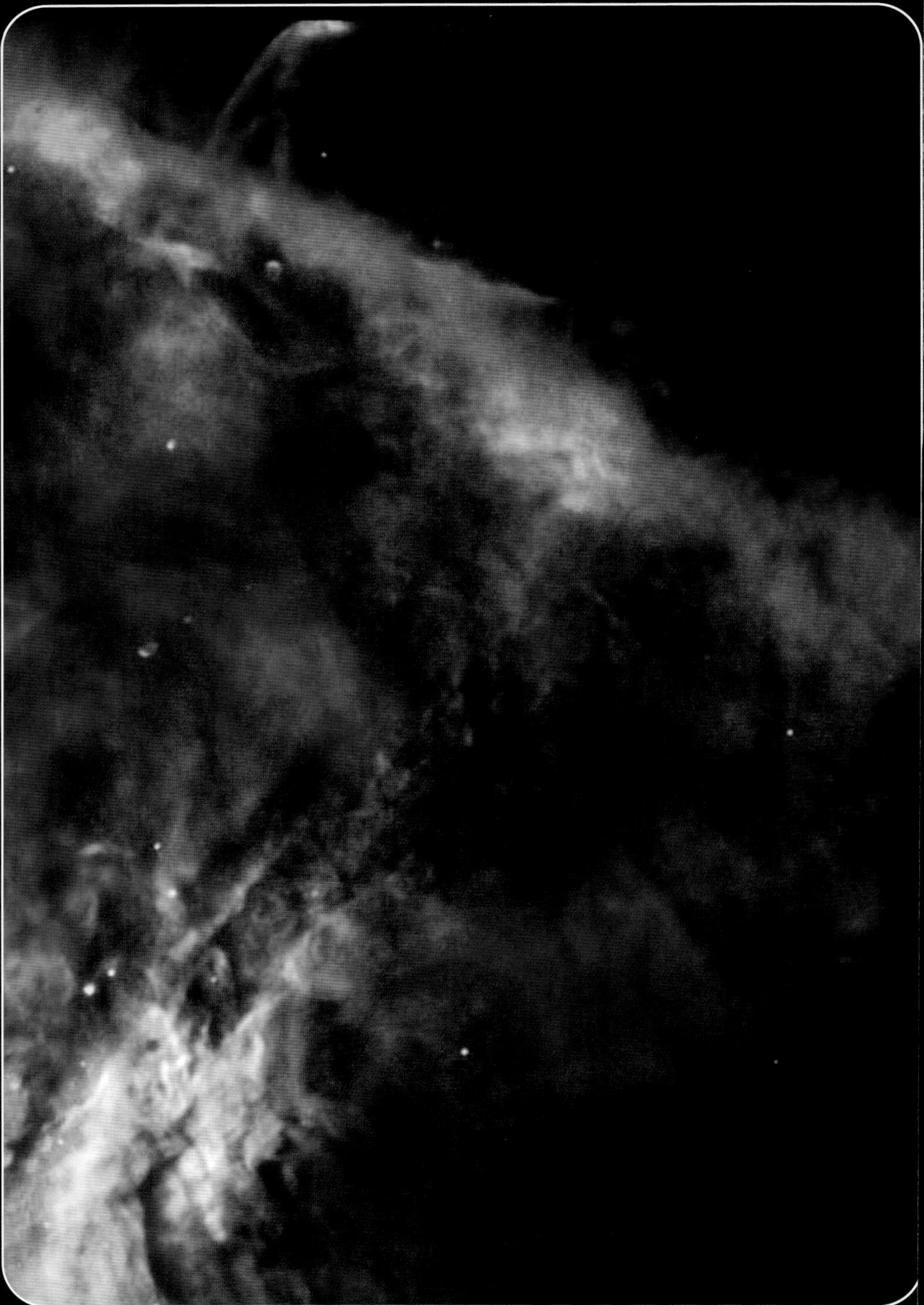

Orion Nebula Gas Plume

NASA's Hubble Space Telescope has uncovered the strongest evidence yet that many stars form planetary systems. Scientists from Rice University in Houston, Texas, have used Hubble to discover extended disks of dust around fifteen newly formed stars in the Orion Nebula, a starbirth region 1,500 light-years away. Such disks are a prerequisite for the formation of solar systems like our own. According to the scientists, "These images provide the best evidence for planetary systems. The disks are a missing link in our understanding of how planets like those in our solar system form. Their discovery establishes that the basic material of planets exists around a large fraction of stars. It is likely that many of these stars will have planetary systems." Hubble Space Telescope's detailed images confirm more than a century of speculation, conjecture, and theory about the genesis of a solar system.

According to current theories, the dust contained within the disks eventually agglomerates to make planets. Our solar system is considered a relic of just such a disk of dust that accompanied our Sun's birth four-and-a-half billion years ago. Before the Hubble discovery, protoplanetary disks had been confirmed around only four stars: Beta Pictoris, Alpha Lyrae, Alpha Piscis Austrini, and Epsilon Eridani. Unlike these previous observations, Hubble has observed newly formed stars less than a million years old which are still contracting out of primordial gas. Hubble's images provide direct evidence that dust surrounding a newborn star has too much spin to be drawn into the collapsing star. Instead the material spreads out into a broad flattened disk.

These young disks signify an entirely new class of object uncovered in the universe. Hubble can see the disks because they are illuminated by the hottest stars in the Orion Nebula; some of them are seen in silhouette against the bright nebula. However, some of these proplyds are bright enough to have been seen previously by ground-based optical and radio telescopes as stars. Their true nature was not recognized until the Hubble discovery. Each proplyd appears as a thick disk with a hole in the middle where the cool star is located. Radiation from nearby hot stars "boils off" material from the disk's surface (at the rate of about one half the mass of our Earth per year). This material is then blown back into a comet-like tail by a stellar "wind" of radiation and subatomic particles streaming from nearby hot stars.

The region of Orion studied intensely by scientists is a bright part of the nebula where stars are being uncovered at the highest rate. These results suggest that nearly half the fifty stars in this part of Orion have protoplanetary disks.

Imagination of Man

Kevlar ~ Stephanie Kwolek
(1966)

Helix Nebula NGC 7293

This cropped version of the Helix Nebula mosaic shows cometary filaments embedded along a portion of the inner rim of the nebula's red-and-blue gas ring. At a distance of 650 light-years, the Helix is one of the nearest planetary nebulae to Earth.

The composite picture is a seamless blend of ultra-sharp NASA Hubble Space Telescope (HST) Advanced Camera for Surveys images combined with the wide view of the Mosaic Camera on the National Science Foundation's 0.9-meter telescope at Kitt Peak National Observatory, part of the National Optical Astronomy Observatory, near Tucson, Arizona. Astronomers at the Space Telescope Science Institute (STScI) assembled the images into a mosaic. The mosaic was blended with a wider photograph taken by the Mosaic Camera.

These features are a forest of thousands of comet-like tentacles that are embedded along the inner rim of the nebula. The tentacles point toward the central star, which is a small but super-hot white dwarf (white dot in the center of the nebula) that seems to float in a sea of blue gas. These tentacles formed when a hot "stellar wind" of gas plowed into colder shells of dust and gas ejected previously by the doomed star.

These comet-like tentacles have been observed from ground-based telescopes for decades, but never have they been seen in such detail. They may actually lie in a disk encircling the hot star, like an animal's collar.

Imagination of Man

Space Flight ~ Soviet Union
(1957)

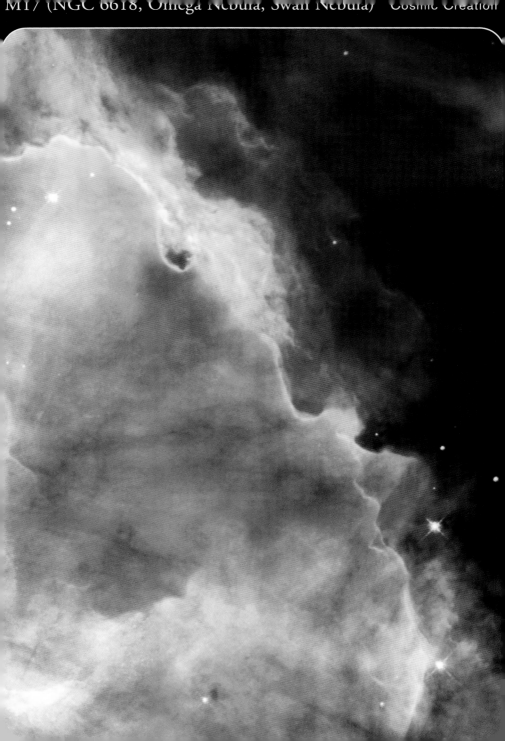

M17 (NGC 6618, Omega Nebula, Swan Nebula)

Resembling the fury of a raging sea, this image actually shows a bubbly ocean of glowing hydrogen gas and small amounts of other elements such as oxygen and sulfur.

The photograph, taken by NASA's Hubble Space Telescope, captures a small region within M17, a hotbed of star formation. M17, also known as the Omega or Swan Nebula, is located about 5,500 light-years away in the constellation Sagittarius. The image is being released to commemorate the thirteenth anniversary of Hubble's launch on April 24, 1990.

The wave-like patterns of gas have been sculpted and illuminated by a torrent of ultraviolet radiation from young massive stars which lie outside the picture to the upper left. The glow of these patterns accentuates the three-dimensional structure of the gases. The ultraviolet radiation is carving and heating the surfaces of cold hydrogen gas clouds. The warmed surfaces glow orange and red in this photograph.

The intense heat and pressure cause some material to stream away from those surfaces, creating the glowing veil of even hotter greenish gas that masks background structures. The pressure on the tips of the waves may trigger new star formations within them.

The image, roughly three light-years across, was taken May 29-30, 1999, with the Wide Field Planetary Camera 2. The colors in the image represent various gases. Red represents sulfur; green, hydrogen; and blue, oxygen.

Imagination of Man

Personal Computer ~ Steve Jobs/Steve Wozniak
(1977)

Eagle Nebula, MI6, NGC 6611

This eerie, dark structure, resembling an imaginary sea serpent's head, is a column of cool molecular hydrogen gas (two atoms of hydrogen in each molecule) and dust that is an incubator for new stars. The stars are embedded inside finger-like protrusions extending from the top of the nebula. Each "fingertip" is somewhat larger than our own solar system.

The pillar is slowly eroding away by the ultraviolet light from nearby hot stars, a process called "photoevaporation." As it does, small globules of especially dense gas buried within the cloud are uncovered. These globules have been dubbed EGGs—an acronym for Evaporating Gaseous Globules. The shadows of the EGGs protect gas behind them, resulting in the finger-like structures at the top of the cloud.

Forming inside at least some of the EGGs are embryonic stars—stars that abruptly stop growing when the EGGs are uncovered and they are separated from the larger reservoir of gas from which they were drawing mass. Eventually the stars emerge, as the EGGs themselves succumb to photoevaporation.

The stellar EGGS are found, appropriately enough, in the "Eagle Nebula" (also called M16—the 16th object in Charles Messier's 18th century catalog of "fuzzy" permanent objects in the sky), a nearby star-forming region 6,500 light-years away in the constellation Serpens.

The picture was taken on April 1, 1995, with the Hubble Space Telescope Wide Field and Planetary Camera 2. The color image is constructed from three separate images taken in the light of emission from different types of atoms. Red shows emission from singly-ionized sulfur atoms. Green shows emission from hydrogen. Blue shows light emitted by doubly ionized oxygen atoms.

Imagination of Man

Theory of Relativity ~ Albert Einstein
(1909)

Spiral Galaxy M74

Resembling festive lights on a holiday wreath, this NASA/ESA Hubble Space Telescope image of the nearby spiral galaxy M74 is an iconic reminder of the Christmas season. Bright knots of glowing gas light up the spiral arms, indicating a rich environment of star formation.

Messier 74, also called NGC 628, is a stunning example of a grand-design spiral galaxy that is viewed by Earth observers nearly face-on. Its perfectly symmetrical spiral arms emanate from the central nucleus and are dotted with clusters of young blue stars and glowing pink regions of ionized hydrogen (hydrogen atoms that have lost their electrons). These regions of star formation show an excess of light at ultraviolet wavelengths. Tracing along the spiral arms are winding dust lanes that also begin very near the galaxy's nucleus and follow along the length of the spiral arms.

M74 is located approximately thirty-two million light-years away in the direction of the constellation Pisces, the Fish. It is the dominant member of a small group of about half a dozen galaxies, the M74 galaxy group. In its entirety, it is estimated that M74 is home to about one hundred billion stars, making it slightly smaller than our Milky Way.

The spiral galaxy was first discovered by the French astronomer Pierre Méchain in 1780. Weeks later it was added to Charles Messier's famous catalog of deep-sky objects.

This Hubble image of M74 is a composite of Advanced Camera for Surveys data taken in 2003 and 2005. The filters used to create the color image isolate light from blue, visible, and infrared portions of the spectrum, as well as emission from ionized hydrogen (known as HII regions).

Imagination of Man

Barbie Doll ~ Ruth Handler
(1959)

Cassiopeia A—Supernova Remnant

An enormous light echo etched in the sky by a fitful dead star was spotted by the infrared eyes of NASA's Spitzer Space Telescope. The surprising finding indicates that Cassiopeia A, the remnant of a star that died in a supernova explosion 325 years ago, is not resting peacefully. Instead, this dead star likely shot out at least one burst of energy as recently as fifty years ago.

"We had thought the stellar remains inside Cassiopeia A were just fading away," said a scientist from the University of Arizona, Tucson. "Spitzer came along and showed us this exploded star, one of the most intensively studied objects in the sky, is still undergoing death throes before heading to its final grave."

Infrared echoes trace the dusty journeys of light waves blasted away from supernova or erupting stars. As the light waves move outward, they heat up clumps of surrounding dust, causing them to glow in infrared light. The echo from Cassiopeia A is the first witnessed around a long-dead star and the largest ever seen. It was discovered by accident during a Spitzer instrument test.

A supernova remnant like Cassiopeia A typically consists of an outer shimmering shell of expelled material and a core skeleton of a once-massive star, called a neutron star. Neutron stars come in several varieties, ranging from intensely active to silent. Typically, a star that has recently died will continue to act up. Consequently, astronomers were puzzled that the star responsible for Cassiopeia A appeared to be silent so soon after its death.

The new infrared echo indicates the Cassiopeia A neutron star is active and may even be an exotic spastic type of object called a "magnetar." Magnetars are like screaming dead stars with eruptive surfaces that rupture and quake, pouring out tremendous amounts of high-energy Gamma rays. Spitzer may have captured the "shriek" of such a star in the form of light zipping away through space and heating up its surroundings.

A close inspection of the Spitzer pictures revealed a blend of at least two light echoes around Cassiopeia A, one from its supernova explosion and one from the hiccup of activity that occurred around 1953. Additional Spitzer observations of these light echoes may help pin down their enigmatic source.

Imagination of Man

Electric Lighting ~Thomas Edison
(1879)

Rho Oph Star-Forming Region

Newborn stars peek out from beneath their natal blanket of dust in this dynamic image of the Rho Ophiuchi dark cloud from NASA's Spitzer Space Telescope.

Called "Rho Oph" by astronomers, it's one of the closest star-forming regions to our own solar system. Located near the constellations Scorpius and Ophiuchus, the nebula is about 407 light-years away from Earth.

Rho Oph is made up of a large main cloud of molecular hydrogen, a key molecule allowing new stars to form out of cold cosmic gas, with two long streamers trailing off in different directions. Recent studies using the latest X-ray and infrared observations reveal more than 300 young stellar objects within the large central cloud. Their median age is only 300,000 years, very young compared to some of the universe's oldest stars, which are more than 12 billion years old.

"Rho Oph is a favorite region for astronomers studying star formation. Because the stars are so young, we can observe them at a very early evolutionary stage, and because the Ophiuchus molecular cloud is relatively close, we can resolve more detail than in more distant clusters, like Orion," said the lead investigator of the new observations, from the Harvard-Smithsonian Center for Astrophysics in Cambridge, Massachusetts. This false-color image of Rho Oph's main cloud, Lynds 1688, was created with data from Spitzer's infrared array camera, which has the highest spatial resolution of Spitzer's three imaging instruments, and its multiband imaging photometer, best for detecting cooler materials.

The colors in this image reflect the relative temperatures and evolutionary states of the various stars. The youngest stars are surrounded by dusty disks of gas from which they and their potential planetary systems are forming. These young disk systems show up as red in this image. Some of these young stellar objects are surrounded by their own compact nebulae. More evolved stars, which have shed their natal material, are blue.

The extended white nebula in the center right of the image is a region of the cloud glowing in infrared light due to the heating of dust by bright young stars near the cloud's right edge. Fainter, multi-hued, diffuse emission fills the image. The color of the nebulosity depends on the temperature, composition, and size of the dust grains. Most of the stars forming now are concentrated in a filament of cold dense gas that shows up as a dark cloud in the lower center and left side of the image against the bright background of the warm dust.

Imagination of Man

Intelligible Telephone ~ Alexander Graham Bell
(1876)

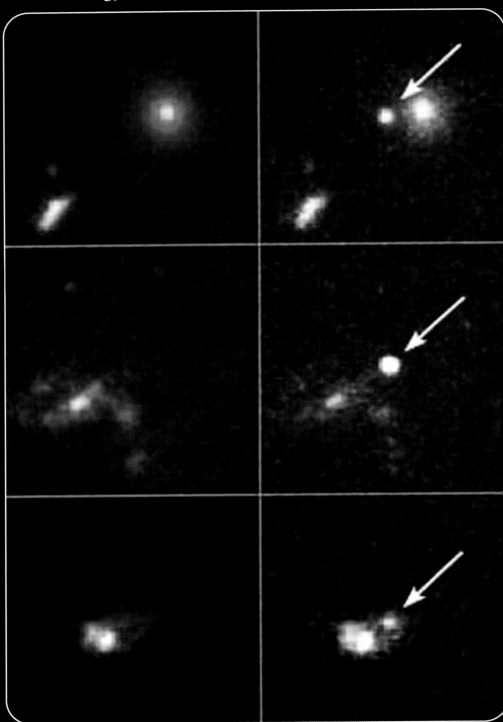

Dark Energy

These are images of three of the most distant supernovae known, discovered using the Hubble Space Telescope as a supernova search engine. The stars exploded back when the universe was approximately half its current age. The light is just arriving at Earth now. Supernovae are so bright they can be seen far away and far back in time. This allows astronomers to trace the expansion rate of the universe, and to determine how it is affected by the repulsive push of dark energy, an unknown form of energy that pervaded space.

WHAT IS DARK ENERGY?

Dark energy is an unknown form of energy that radiates from deep space. It behaves in the opposite manner from gravity. Rather than pulling galaxies together it pushes them apart.

DID ANYONE PREDICT DARK ENERGY?

Dark energy is a complete surprise. However, Albert Einstein theorized the existence of a repulsive form of gravity in space that would balance the universe against normal gravity and keep it from imploding. Einstein called it the "cosmological constant."

HOW DOES DARK ENERGY AFFECT THE UNIVERSE?

Dark energy makes up the bulk of the universe's mass/energy budget. If dark energy is stable the universe will continue expanding and accelerating forever. If dark energy is unstable the universe could ultimately come unglued to the point where stars, planets, and even atoms come apart, a doomsday scenario called the "big rip." Dark energy might also flip such that it becomes an attractive force and causes the universe to implode in a "big crunch."

HOW CAN HUBBLE "SEE" DARK ENERGY?

Hubble can measure the faint glow of distant supernovae, stars that exploded billions of years ago. Supernovae trace the expansion history of the universe, hence, how dark energy "pushed" on space over the past epochs. Every second a star explodes somewhere in the universe, so it's a matter of Hubble looking in the right place at the right time.

DOES HUBBLE PROVE HOW DARK ENERGY REALLY BEHAVES?

These latest Hubble observations show that dark energy is not changing its behavior over time, and so may be the "constant" Einstein predicted. However, more observations are needed over the coming decade.

Imagination of Man

Practical Typewriter ~ Christopher Sholes / Carlos Glidden
(1867)

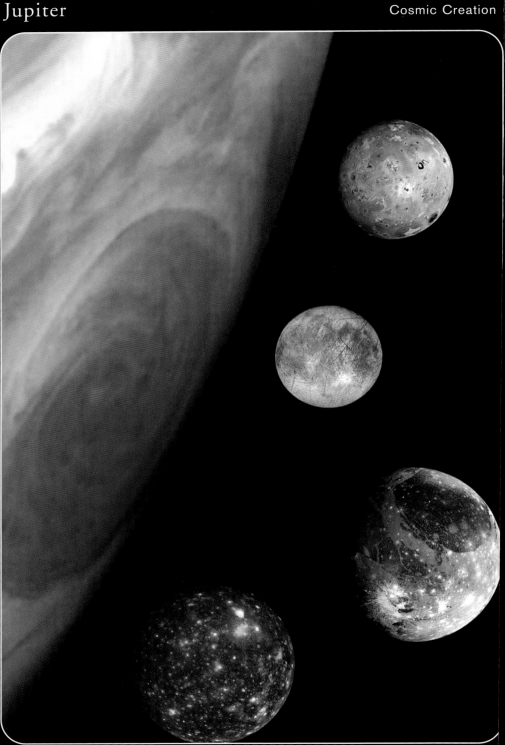

Jupiter

The most massive planet in our solar system, with four planet-sized moons and many smaller moons, Jupiter forms a kind of miniature solar system. Jupiter resembles a star in composition. In fact, if it had been about eighty times more massive, it would have become a star rather than a planet.

On January 7, 1610, using his primitive telescope, astronomer Galileo Galilei saw four small "stars" near Jupiter. He had discovered Jupiter's four largest moons, now called *Io, Europa, Ganymede,* and *Callisto.* Collectively, these four moons are known today as the Galilean satellites.

Galileo would be astonished at what we have learned about Jupiter and its moons in the past thirty years. Io is the most volcanically active body in our solar system. Ganymede is the largest planetary moon and is the only moon in the solar system known to have its own magnetic field. A liquid ocean may lie beneath the frozen crust of Europa. Icy oceans may also lie deep beneath the crusts of Callisto and Ganymede. In 2003 alone, astronomers discovered twenty-three new moons orbiting the giant planet, giving Jupiter a total moon count of forty-nine officially named—the most in the solar system. The numerous small outer moons may be asteroids captured by the giant planet's gravity. Jupiter's appearance is a tapestry of beautiful colors and atmospheric features. Most visible clouds are composed of ammonia. Water exists deep below and can sometimes be seen through clear spots in the clouds. The planet's "stripes" are dark belts and light zones created by strong east-west winds in Jupiter's upper atmosphere. Within these belts and zones are storm systems that have raged for years. The Great Red Spot, a giant spinning storm, has been observed for more than 300 years.

The composition of Jupiter's atmosphere is similar to that of the Sun—mostly hydrogen and helium. Deep in the atmosphere, the pressure and temperature increase, compressing the hydrogen gas into a liquid. At depths about a third of the way down, the hydrogen becomes metallic and electrically conducting. In this metallic layer, Jupiter's powerful magnetic field is generated by electrical currents driven by Jupiter's fast rotation. At the center, the immense pressure may support a solid core of ice-rock about the size of Earth. Jupiter's enormous magnetic field is nearly 20,000 times as powerful as the Earth's. Trapped within Jupiter's magnetosphere (the area in which magnetic field lines encircle the planet from pole to pole) are swarms of charged particles. Jupiter's rings and moons are embedded in an intense radiation belt of electrons and ions trapped in the magnetic field.

Imagination of Man

Father of Modern Observational Astronomy ~ Galileo
(1564-1692)

Galaxy Centaurus A

A dramatic new Chandra image of the nearby galaxy Centaurus A provides one of the best views to date of the effects of an active supermassive black hole. Opposing jets of high-energy particles can be seen extending to the outer reaches of the galaxy, and numerous smaller black holes in binary star systems are also visible. The image was made from an ultra-deep look at the galaxy Centaurus A, equivalent to more than seven days of continuous observations. Centaurus A is the nearest galaxy to Earth that contains a supermassive black hole actively powering a jet. A prominent X-ray jet extending for 13,000 light-years points to the upper left in the image, with a shorter "counterjet" aimed in the opposite direction. Astronomers think that such jets are important vehicles for transporting energy from the black hole to the much larger dimensions of a galaxy, and affecting the rate at which stars form there. High-energy electrons spiraling around magnetic field lines produce the X-ray emission from the jet and counterjet. This emission quickly saps the energy from the electrons, so they must be continually reaccelerated or the X-rays will fade out. Knot-like features in the jets detected in the Chandra image show where the acceleration of particles to high energies is currently occurring, and provides important clues to understanding the process that accelerates the electrons to near-light speeds.

The inner part of the X-ray jet close to the black hole is dominated by these knots of X-ray emission, which probably come from shock waves—akin to sonic booms—caused by the jet. Farther from the black hole there is more diffuse X-ray emission in the jet. The cause of particle acceleration in this part of the jet is unknown. Hundreds of point-like sources are also seen in the Chandra image. Many of these are X-ray binaries that contain a stellar-mass black hole and a companion star in orbit around one another. Determining the population and properties of these black holes should help scientists better understand the evolution of massive stars and the formation of black holes.

Another surprise was the detection of two particularly bright X-ray binaries. These sources may contain stellar mass black holes that are unusually massive, and this Chandra observation might have caught them gobbling up material at a high rate.

In this image, low-energy X-rays are colored red, intermediate-energy X-rays are green, and the highest-energy X-rays detected by Chandra are blue. The dark-green and blue bands running almost perpendicular to the jet are dust lanes that absorb X-rays. This dust lane was created when Centaurus A merged with another galaxy perhaps 100 million years ago.

Imagination of Man

Microscope ~ Hans and Zacharias Janssen
(1590)

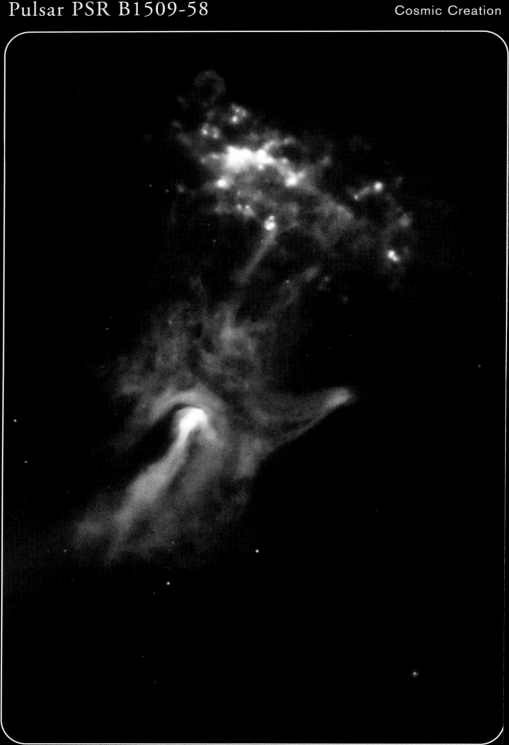

Pulsar PSR B1509-58

A small, dense object only twelve miles in diameter is responsible for this beautiful X-ray nebula that spans 150 light-years. At the center of this image made by NASA's Chandra X-ray Observatory is a very young and powerful pulsar, known as PSR B1509-58, or B1509 for short. The pulsar is a rapidly spinning neutron star which is spewing energy out into the space around it to create complex and intriguing structures, including one that resembles a large cosmic hand. In this image, the lowest energy X-rays that Chandra detects are colored red, the medium range is green, and the most energetic ones are blue. Astronomers think that B1509 is about 1,700 years old as measured in Earth's time-frame (referring to when events are observable at Earth) and is located about 17,000 light years away.

Neutron stars are created when massive stars run out of fuel and collapse. B1509 is spinning completely around almost seven times every second and is releasing energy into its environment at a prodigious rate—presumably because it has an intense magnetic field at its surface, estimated to be 15 trillion times stronger than the Earth's magnetic field.

The combination of rapid rotation and an ultra-strong magnetic field makes B1509 one of the most powerful electromagnetic generators in the Galaxy. This generator drives an energetic wind of electrons and ions away from the neutron star. As the electrons move through the magnetized nebula, they radiate away their energy and create the elaborate nebula seen by Chandra.

In the innermost regions, a faint circle surrounds the pulsar, and marks the spot where the wind is rapidly decelerated by the slowly expanding nebula. In this way, B1509 shares some striking similarities to the famous Crab Nebula. However B1509's nebula is fifteen times wider than the Crab's diameter of ten light-years.

Finger-like structures extend to the north, apparently energizing knots of material in a neighboring gas cloud known as RCW 89. The transfer of energy from the wind to these knots makes them glow brightly in X-rays (orange and red features to the upper right). The temperature in this region appears to vary in a circular pattern around this ring of emission, suggesting that the pulsar may be processing like a spinning top and sweeping an energizing beam around the gas in RCW 89. (This image has been called the "Hand of God" by some.)

Imagination of Man

Jet Propulsion ~ Hans Joachim Pabst von Ohain
(1936)

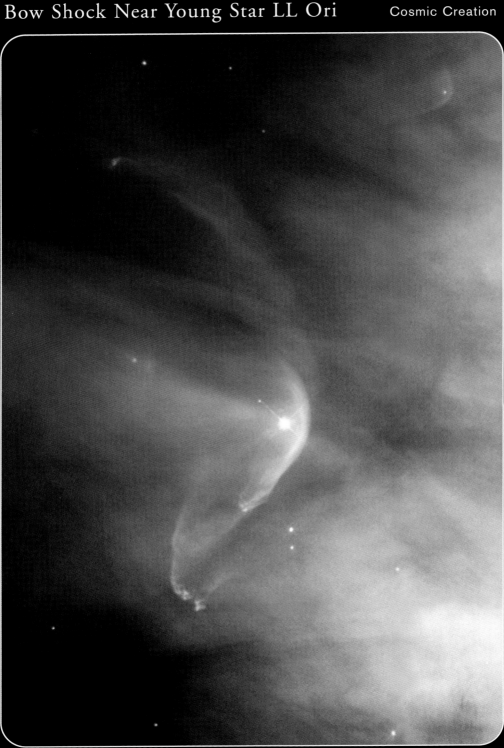

Bow Shock Near Young Star LL Ori

NASA's Hubble Space Telescope continues to reveal various stunning and intricate treasures that reside within the nearby, intense, star-forming region known as the Great Nebula in Orion. One such jewel is the bow shock around the very young star, LL Ori, featured in this Hubble Heritage image.

Named for the crescent-shaped wave made by a ship as it moves through water, a bow shock can be created in space when two streams of gas collide. LL Ori emits a vigorous solar wind, a stream of charged particles moving rapidly outward from the star. Our own Sun has a less energetic version of this wind that is responsible for auroral displays on the Earth.

The material in the fast wind from LL Ori collides with slow-moving gas evaporating away from the center of the Orion Nebula, which is located to the lower right in this Heritage image. The surface where the two winds collide is the crescent-shaped bow shock seen in the image.

Unlike a water wave made by a ship, this interstellar bow shock is a three-dimensional structure. The filamentary emission has a very distinct boundary on the side facing away from LL Ori, but is diffuse on the side closest to the star, a characteristic common to many bow shocks.

A second, fainter bow shock can be seen around a star near the upper right-hand corner of the Heritage image. Astronomers have identified numerous shock fronts in this complex star-forming region and are using this data to understand the many complex phenomena associated with the birth of stars.

This image was taken in February 1995 as part of the Hubble Orion Nebula mosaic. A close visitor in our Milky Way galaxy, the nebula is only 1,500 light-years from Earth. The filters used in this color composite represent oxygen, nitrogen, and hydrogen emissions.

Imagination of Man

Penicillin ~ Sir Alexander Fleming
(1928)

Hubble Ultra Deep Field

Galaxies, galaxies everywhere—as far as NASA's Hubble Space Telescope can see. This view of nearly 10,000 galaxies is the deepest visible-light image of the cosmos. Called the Hubble Ultra Deep Field, this galaxy-studded view represents a "deep" core sample of the universe, cutting across billions of light-years.

The snapshot includes galaxies of various ages, sizes, shapes, and colors. The smallest, reddest galaxies, about 100, may be among the most distant known, existing when the universe was just 800 million years old. The nearest galaxies—the larger, brighter, well-defined spirals and ellipticals—thrived about one billion years ago, when the cosmos was 13 billion years old.

In vibrant contrast to the rich harvest of classic spiral and elliptical galaxies, there is a zoo of oddball galaxies littering the field. Some look like toothpicks; others like links on a bracelet. A few appear to be interacting. These oddball galaxies chronicle a period when the universe was younger and more chaotic. Order and structure were just beginning to emerge.

The Ultra Deep Field observations, taken by the Advanced Camera for Surveys, represent a narrow, deep view of the cosmos. Peering into the Ultra Deep Field is like looking through an eight-foot-long soda straw.

In ground-based photographs, the patch of sky in which the galaxies reside (just one-tenth the diameter of the full Moon) is largely empty. Located in the constellation Fornax, the region is so empty that only a handful of stars within the Milky Way galaxy can be seen in the image.

In this image, blue and green correspond to colors that can be seen by the human eye, such as hot, young, blue stars and the glow of Sun-like stars in the disks of galaxies. Red represents near-infrared light, which is invisible to the human eye, such as the red glow of dust-enshrouded galaxies.

The image required 800 exposures taken over the course of 400 Hubble orbits around Earth. The total amount of exposure time was 11.3 days, taken between September 24, 2003, and January 16, 2004.

Imagination of Man

Hubble Space Telescope ~ NASA
(1990)

ACKNOWLEDGMENTS

I WOULD LIKE TO THANK NASA AND THE ASSOCIATED ORGANIZATIONS MENtioned in the credits section of this book that are responsible for the Hubble, Spitzer, and other telescopes. None of these photos would be available without their hard work and dedication.

Thank you to everyone who wrote background information on these findings from Hubble and Spitzer, to help us better understand how this grand universe is unfolding before us. The world is grateful to all the men and women who have dedicated their lives to bring into view the Grandest Drama of all time, some even at the cost of their own lives. You are performing a valuable service for a noble cause to *"Look up into the heavens"* and see *"Who created all the stars?"*

I would like to acknowledge Mary Jo Zazueta of To The Point Solutions for her skillful work on the interior design, David Yanor for his work on the glossary and editing, and Brion Sausser for the cover design. Thanks also to Zoom Astronomy at Enchanted Learning, and the hard-workign people at Cal Tech.

Finally, and most importantly, I thank my wife, Diane, for her love and patience during this project and my daughters, Crystal, Tara, and Megan, for their love and for just being themselves. You all mean the world to me.

Also, I want to thank my sisters, Rose Mary, Rita, Rhonda, and Renee, for their helpful input and encouragement; and thank you to my friends who read the manuscript and gave me feedback.

ABOUT THE AUTHOR

FROM TROUBLED TEEN TO A SUCCESSFUL ENTREPRENEUR and author, J. Paul Hutchins' story began when, as a terrified nineteen-year-old, he found himself cowering in a passenger seat, covering his head, and silently praying the rural Kentucky sheriff's bullets would miss their mark and he would make it out alive. As his friend pursued an escape, the teens flew down a country road at potentially lethal speeds. Scared for his life, the high-speed chase was the beginning of a personal life change and the catalyst that would change the course of his life, eventually leading him to write *Hubble Reveals Creation.*

Following his father's death at age thirteen, Hutchins, one of ten siblings, lacked guidance and motivation. With his mother working full-time to support the large family, he was left without a father figure and adequate parental guidance. As a teenager, Hutchins became involved with illegal drugs, petty crime, and delinquency. It wasn't until he found himself in the high-speed chase, riding passenger to a prison-bound friend that he realized something needed to change. Unable to sync his thoughts with reality and lacking a sense of purpose, he considered suicide.

On drugs at age ninenteen, Hutchins began to evaluate his life and resolved to go in a new direction, which saved him from following his brother to prison—who was later shot and killed. His friend from the high-speed chase was later featured on *America's Most Wanted* for double murder.

"Many of the friends I ran with in those days are dead from either a drug overdose or suicide," Hutchins says. "A good majority went to prison."

Today, Hutchins is a successful entrepreneur and says he's fortunate to be alive. A patented inventor and amateur astronomer, he began to notice the role imagination played in every major discovery in man's history. As he set out to explore the imagination of man, his search led him to consider the universe and its design—stars, galaxies, nebulas, planets—all of which Hutchins says are the result of One supreme imagination.

After researching the images and data from the Hubble and Spritzer space telescopes, collected since their launch, Hutchins was compelled to write about the universe as a product of intelligent design, fueled by Superior Imagination. In his new book, *Hubble Reveals Creation by an Awe-Inspiring Power*, Hutchins stitches together a photographic drama of the creation of the universe, examining the intricacies of the universe and invoking a Grand Architect as the creative force behind our world. With full-color photos, scientific data, and a user-friendly format, Hutchins takes readers on an awe-inspiring journey as he considers what lies beyond imagination.

The parents of three adult daughters, Hutchins and his wife currently reside in Orlando, Florida.

For more information go to:
http://www.HubbleRevealsCreation.com

GLOSSARY

Adaptive Optics: Technology used to improve the performance of optical systems by reducing the effect of wavefront distortions.

Andromeda Galaxy: This is a major spiral galaxy, 2.2 million light-years from Earth. Gravitationally bound to the Milky Way galaxy with which it shares membership in the Local Group.

Anisotropies: Small fluctuations in the temperature of the CMB in the blackbody radiation left over from the Big Bang.

Antennae Galaxies (NGC 4038-4039): A merging pair of galaxies. A famous pair of interacting galaxies in the constellation Corvus. Each galaxy's tidal force has drawn out a long tail of stars from the other. The Antennae are also known as NGC 4038 and NGC 4039.

Apollo Space Program: Successful U. S. lunar exploration program in which the Apollo spacecraft 1 to 6 were unmanned; 7 to 10 were manned but did not land; and 11, 12 and 14 to 17 landed and returned safely. The final Apollo flight (17) lasted from 7 to 19 December 1972, and left a considerable quantity of exploratory devices on the lunar surface.

Astronomical Interferometer: An array of telescopes or mirror segments acting together to probe structures with higher resolution by means of interferometry.

Astrophysical Masers: Naturally occurring microwave and radio-wave emissions that provide an important tool to investigate astrophysical environments.

Barred Spiral Galaxy: One whose center is elongated and spiral, or bar-shaped. A spiral galaxy whose nucleus is in the shape of a bar, at the ends of which the spiral arms start.

Barred Spiral Galaxy (NGC 1300): Located sixty-nine million light-years away, in the direction of the constellation Eridanus.

Big Bang Theory: This theory postulates that the universe began as a tiny but intense explosion almost fourteen billion years ago. An evolutionary model of cosmology in which the universe began in a state of extremely high density and temperature. According to this model, the universe has been expanding, thinning out, and cooling since its beginning.

Biomimicry: looking to nature for design inspiration, such as with photosynthesis, natural selection and self-sustaining ecosystems.

Black Hole: A massive region in space that is so dense within its radius that its gravitational field does not let anything escape from it, not even light. Scientists theorize that the average black hole is ten times larger than our Sun.

Bubble Nebula (NGC 7635): Ten light-years wide, it is located in the constellation Cassiopeia.

Cassiopeia: Cassiopeia is an easily seen constellation that is in the far northern sky. It circles the polestar (Polaris) throughout the year and also straddles the Milky Way.

Cat's Eye Nebula (NGC 6543): Considered one of the most complex planetary nebula yet discovered, the photos show intricate structures and lots of evidence of gas in many forms. Cat's Eye is about 3,000 light-years away from Earth.

Centaurus A Galaxy (NGC 1528): This provides one of the best views of an active supermassive black hole. It is the nearest known violent galaxy.

Chandra X-Ray Observatory: This is the world's most powerful X-ray telescope. It orbits around the Earth. It is a forty-five foot satellite that records X-rays from high-energy parts of the sky. It was launched on the Space Shuttle Columbia on July 23, 1999.

(CMB) Microwave Background Radiation: The remnant energy left over from the formation of the universe, according to the Big Bang theory.

Cone Nebula (NGC 2264): A conical shaped conglomeration of gas and dust, it is twenty-five hundred light-years away.

Constellation: A group of stars, which, when viewed from Earth, seem to form some pattern.

Copernicus, Nicolaus (1473-1543): He was an amateur Polish astronomer who developed the revolutionary Copernican system, a model of the solar system in which all the planets orbit the Sun. His ideas overturned the old Ptolemaic System.

Cosmic: Of or relating to the cosmos, the extraterrestrial vastness, or the universe in contrast to the earth alone. Cosmos is an orderly or harmonious system.

Crab Nebula (NGC 1952): The Crab Nebula (M1) is a cloud of intergalactic gas and dust. It is the remnant of a supernova that was seen on Earth in 1054. The Crab Nebula can be found in the constellation Taurus.

Cygnus: A constellation six hundred light-years from Earth. Cygnus (the swan) is shaped like a large cross. It is also known as the Northern Cross. It is seen along the Milky Way in the northern hemisphere.

Danger Zones: If star dust and gases are too close to a new hot star, they risk losing their star- and planet-making capability due to the radiation and winds generated by the new (or O) star.

Dark Energy: This nebulous form of matter makes up the vast bulk of deep space. It repels rather than attracts, unlike gravity. Some astronomers see this as a wild card that may not be predicted.

Eagle Nebula (M16 NGC 6611): It consists of enormous columns of cool interstellar hydrogen gas and dust that are about 7,000 light-years from Earth, in the constellation Serpens.

Elephant's Trunk Nebula: In the constellation Cepheus, 2450 light-years from the Earth.

Eskimo Nebula (NGC 2392): It resembles a face in a parka. It is located about 5,000 light-years from Earth in the constellation Gemini. The Eskimo Nebula is a plantary nebula in Gemini. It is a dying sun-like star, whose outer layers have begun to drift off into space. It was first sighted by William Herschel in 1787.

Extrasolar Planets: Planets outside our solar system.

Gagarin, Yuri (1934-1968): He became the first human to view Earth from space. He was a Soviet cosmonaut and the first man to orbit the Earth. He piloted the Vostok 1 mission which launched April 12, 1961, and orbited the Earth. The flight lasted 108 minutes.

Galaxy: A galaxy is a huge group of stars and other celestial bodies bound together by gravitational forces. There are spiral, elliptical, and irregularly shaped galaxies. Our Sun and solar system are a small part of the Milky Way galaxy.

Galilei, Galileo (1564-1642): An Italian mathematician, astronomer, and physicist. Galileo found that the speed at which bodies fall does not depend on their weight and did extensive experimentation with pendulums. In 1609, Galileo was the first person to use a telescope to observe the skies (after hearing about Hans Lippershey's newly invented telescope).

Gamma-rays: Electromagnetic radiation of high frequency (very short wavelength). They are produced by subatomic particle interactions.

Gamma-ray Burst Events: Flashes of Gamma-rays associated with extremely energetic explosions in distant galaxies. They are the most luminous electromagnetic events occurring in the universe.

Halo: This is a luminous ring that is sometimes seen surrounding the Sun or the Moon. Some parts of the halo are very bright; others are not very bright. The halo is produced as light is reflected and refracted through tiny, flat ice crystals in the atmosphere.

HD Number: The HD (Henry Draper) number is an identifying number assigned to the stars in the Henry Draper catalog. In this system, every star is classified by its stellar spectrum.

Heliocentrism: A concept whereby the Sun is the center of our planetary system, with all the planets revolving around the Sun.

Helix Nebula (NGC 7293): This is a planetary nebula that has the largest angular diameter of any known planetary nebula. It is about 700 light-years or 140 parsecs away, in Aquarius. There is a dead star at the center of this nebula, providing an eerie glow that resembles an eye, with the dust surrounding it.

Henize 206: Located within the Large Magellanic Cloud in the Southern Hemisphere, it is considered an ideal cosmic laboratory that may resemble the distant universe in its chemical composition.

Hipparcos: The European Space Agency's satellite. It has claimed to have pinpointed more than 100 000 stars, 200 times more accurately than ever before.

Hubble, Edwin Powell (1889-1953): An American astronomer who was very influential in modern cosmology. He showed that other galaxies (besides the Milky Way) existed and observed that the universe is expanding (since the light from almost all other galaxies is red-shifted).

Hubble Space Telescope (HST): A powerful telescope in orbit around the Earth. HST transmits pictures and spectra of objects in space without the interference of the atmosphere (which makes telescopic images from the ground have less detail). It was launched into space in April 1990 and was repaired in December 1993. It was named for the American astronomer Edwin Hubble.

Infrared radiation: Infrared radiation is electromagnetic radiation that we can feel as heat.

Interferometry: Refers to a family of techniques in which electromagnetic waves are superimposed in order to extract information about the waves.

Isotropic: An isotropic radiator is a theoretical point source of electromagnetic or sound waves which radiates the same intensity of radiation in all directions.

Jupiter: The largest planet in our solar system, Jupiter has four larger and many smaller moons orbiting it. Scientists have discovered forty-nine so far. Its magnetic field is about twenty thousand times stronger than that of the Earth's.

Kuiper, Gerard Peter (1905-1973): A Dutch-American astronomer who predicted the existence of the Kuiper belt in 1951.

Kuiper Belt: A stable debris disc, filled with comets, in the Milky Way galaxy. A region beyond Neptune in which at least 70,000 small objects (KBO's) orbit, including Quaoar and Sedna. This belt was discovered in 1992.

Magellanic Clouds: Irregular-shaped galaxies, congregations of millions of stars. The irregular shape may be the result of a disturbance, perhaps a collision of two galaxies.

Mars: One of the closest planets which has fired man's imagination. It is termed the "red planet," the fourth planet from the Sun.

Megaparsec (Mpc): A unit of distance that is equal to one million parsecs, 3.26 x 106 light-years or 3.085678 x1019 kilometers. The Local Group of galaxies is roughly a megaparsec in diameter.

Microgravity Environment: An environment where gravity has little or no measurable effect.

Milky Way galaxy: A spiral galaxy—our Sun and solar system are a small part of it. Most of the stars that we can see are in the Milky Way galaxy. The main plane of the Milky Way looks like a faint band of white in the night sky. The Milky Way is about 100,000 light-years in diameter and 1,000 light-years thick.

Molecular Clouds: Sometimes called a stellar nursery if star formation is occurring within, is a type of interstellar cloud whose density and size permits the formation of molecules, most commonly molecular hydrogen. The only places where star formation (and planet formation) is known to occur.

Monoceros Light Echo (V8383): We find these spirals of dust 20,000 light-years from Earth. At one point it was 600,000 more luminous than out Sun, but then it faded away.

Nanometer: A unit of length in the metric system, equal to one billionth of a meter.

NASA: The National Aeronautics and Space Administration. It is the governmental agency that oversees space exploration for the USA.

National Oceanic and Atmospheric Administration's AVHRR sensor: the Advanced Very High Resolution Radiometer.

Nebula: A huge, diffuse cloud of gas and dust in intergalactic space. The gas in nebulae (the plural of nebula) is mostly hydrogen gas (H_2).

Neutron Star: A very small, super-dense star which is composed mostly of tightly packed neutrons. This hard-to-see body has a thin atmosphere of super-hot hydrogen plasma and a crust. It has a diameter of about 5-10 miles (5-16 kilometers) and a density of roughly 10 15 gm/cm3. Neutron stars are formed from supernova explosions. Also called a "magnestar."

Newton, Isaac (1642-1727): An English mathematician and physicist who invented calculus (simultaneously, but independently of Leibniz), formulated the laws of gravitation, investigated the nature of light. He discovered that sunlight is made of light of different colors. He also formulated the laws of motion. Newton also improved the design of the refracting telescope (using an objective mirror instead of a lens), and it is now called a Newtonian Telescope.

NGC (New General Catalog): A list of over 13,000 deep-sky celestial objects. It was developed in 1888 by John Dreyer. For example, the Great Nebula in Orion is NCG 1976 (and M42). NGC4414 is a spiral galaxy 60 million light-years away.

NGC 602: *see* Small Magellanic Cloud.

NGC 2440 Planetary Nebula: A white dwarf dwells at the centre of this nebula. It has a great deal of dust and gas and is located in the constellation Puppis, 4,000 light-years from Earth.

NGC 5194: A compact galaxy that has been passing behind the Whirlpool galaxy for hundreds of millions of years.

Nuclear Fission: A reaction in which an atom's nucleus is broken apart, releasing a tremendous amount of energy.

Nuclear Fusion: an atomic reaction in which many nuclei (the centers of atoms) combine together to make a larger one (which is a different element). The result of this process is the release of a lot of energy (the resultant nucleus is smaller in mass than the sum of the ones that made it).

Omega Nebula, Swan Nebula (NGC 6618, M17): Located about 5,500 light-years from Earth, this is a hotbed of star formation.

Ophiuchus Constellation (pronounced OFF-ee-YOOkuss): or "snake carrier" constellation about 375 light-years from Earth.

Orion: It is also known as "The Hunter," is a constellation. The brightest stars in Orion are Rigel, Betelgeuse, and Bellatrix. The Horsehead Nebula and the nebulae M42 and M43 (called the Orion nebula) are also in this constellation.

Orion Nebula (M42, NGC 1976): The Orion Nebula (M42 and M43) is a huge, nearby, turbulent gas cloud (mostly hydrogen) that is lit up by bright, young, hot stars (including the asterism called Trapezium) that are developing within the nebula. This nebula is located about 1,500 light-years away from us towards the constellation of Orion.

O-star: O-type stars are massive, bright, hot stars. They are the bluest of the of the main sequence stars.

Parallax Measurements: Astronomers use an effect called parallax to measure distances to nearby stars.

Parsec: Astronomical unit of distance equal to 3.26 light-years.

Perseus constellation: Perseus is a constellation in the Milky Way in the Northern Hemisphere.

Photoevaporation: denotes the process when a planet is stripped of its atmosphere due to high energy photons and other electromagnetic radiation.

Photometric Photography: Photometry is a technique of astronomy concerned with measuring the flux, or intensity, of an astronomical object's electromagnetic radiation.

Planck Time: The first instant following the beginning of the expansion of the Universe, when the cosmic matter density was still so high that gravitational force acted as strongly as the other fundamental forces on the subatomic scale.

Planetary Nebulae: Glowing shrouds surrounding Sun-like stars. A planetary nebula is a nebula formed by a shell of gas which was ejected from a certain kind of extremely hot star. As the giant star explodes, the core of the star is exposed.

Pleiades Star Cluster (M45): Also known as the Seven Sisters (and "Subaru" in Japan), though about one thousand stars actually make up the cluster. It is located in the constellation Taurus. It is estimated that it is about 440 light-years from Earth. It is the brightest open cluster of stars in the sky.

Polycyclic Aromatic Hydrocarbons (PAH): comprised of carbon and hydrogen. The molecules are considered to be among the building blocks of life.

Proplyds: *See* **Protoplanetary Disks**.

Protoplanetary Disks: Birthplace of stars and planets. Also called "proplyds," they are the building blocks of solar systems. A protoplanetary disk is a rotating disk of dust that surrounds the central core of a developing solar system. This disk eventually coalesces into planets that orbit the star (which forms from the central core).

Proxima Centauri: Our Sun's closest star, nearly thirty trillion miles away.

Protostars: A protostar is a star that is still forming and nuclear fusion has not yet begun.

Quasars: A Quasar is a very energetic and distant active galactic nucleus. Quasars are extremely bright masses of energy and light.

RCW 49: Located 13,700 light-years away in a southern constellation, Centaurus. It has a reputation for being a fertile breeding ground for new stars, with more than twenty-two hundred in its "stellar nursery."

Reflection Nebula (NGC 1999): A nebula located in the constellation Orion. It is illuminated by a young star that is so hot, it is white in color. Much hotter and almost four times larger than our Sun.

Reflection Nebula (NGC 7129): Located 3,300 light-years from Earth in the constellation Cepheus, it has approximately 130 young stars within its folds. A reflection nebula is a nebula that glows as the dust in it reflects the light of nearby stars.

Rho Oph Star-Forming Region: This region is about 407 light-years from Earth, relatively close. It contains more than 300 young stars that are a mere three hundred thousand years old.

Rosette Nebula: Found in the constellation Monoceros, this nebula looks like a rosebud, but those are super-hot stars, termed O-stars, that are providing the light and heat.

Scorpius: Scorpius (the scorpion) is a constellation of the zodiac. This constellation is seen along the ecliptic between Libra and Sagittarius.

Small Magellanic Cloud (NGC 602): In the constellation Tucana it is about 200,000 light-years from the Earth. It is known as an older dwarf galaxy, with many fewer stars than our galaxy.

Sombrero Galaxy (M104): The galaxy's hallmark is a brilliant-white bulbous core encircled by the thick dust lanes comprising the spiral structure of the galaxy. As seen from Earth, the galaxy is tilted nearly edge-on . . . This brilliant galaxy was named the Sombrero because of its resemblance to the broad rim and hightopped Mexican hat.

Space Infrared Telescope Facility (SIRTF): an infrared cousin of the Hubble Space Telescope that followed Hubble into space in 2003. Spitzer detects infrared, longer wavelength light that our eyes cannot see. It detects the infrared energy, or heat, radiated by objects in space and is able to detect dust disks around stars.

Spectroscopes: Break down the light emitted or absorbed by chemical elements into specific lines of color. Each element has an indefinable fingerprint.

Spectroscopic Analysis: Analysis of a spectrum to determine characteristics of its source; for example, analysis of the optical spectrum of a luminous body to determine its composition or motion.

Spectroscopy: The study of the absorption and emission of light and other radiation, by matter.

Speed of Light: The speed at which electromagnetic waves can move in a vacuum = 186,000 miles per second. According to Einstein's theory of relativity, nothing can go faster than the speed of light.

Spiral Galaxy (M74, NGC 628): A grand-design spiral galaxy thirty-two million light-years away in the Pisces constellation. It is home to about a hundred billion stars, slightly fewer than those in our own Milky Way galaxy.

Spirographic Nebula (IC 418): This planetary nebula lies some 2,000 light-years from Earth in the direction of the constellation Lepus.

Spitzer Space Telescope: The Spitzer Space Telescope (formerly SIRTF, the Space Infrared Telescope Facility) was launched into space by a Delta rocket from Cape Canaveral, Florida, on August 25, 2003. During its mission, Spitzer will obtain images and spectra by detecting the infrared energy, or heat, radiated by objects in space between wavelengths of 3 and 180 microns (1 micron is one-millionth of a meter). Most of this infrared radiation is blocked by the Earth's atmosphere and cannot be observed from the ground.

Standard Candles: Stars used to measure more distant, fainter stars. An object—usually a star or a galaxy of known intrinsic brightness. Measuring the apparent brightness of a standard candle yields its distance.

Star: Each star in the sky is a glowing ball of gas. Our Sun is a medium-sized star. The first stars in the Universe appeared about 200 million years after the Big Bang (which occurred about 13.7 billon years ago).

Star Cluster: A group of stars positioned close together in space. A gravitationally bound aggregation of stars, smaller and less massive than galaxies. "Globular" clusters are the largest category; they are old, and may harbor hundreds of thousands to millions of stars, and are found both within and well away from the galactic disk.

Steady-State Theory: Some scientists believe that the universe always has been and always will be as it is. They say that the universe is not expanding and is uniform and infinite.

Sun: The center of our solar system, the Sun is the closest star to Earth, approximately ninety-four million miles from Earth. It is comprised mostly of ionized gas and is massive: 332,900 times larger than Earth.

Sunspot: Comparatively dark spot on the Sun's photosphere, commonly one of a (not always obvious) group of two. The center of a vast electrostatic field and a magnetic field of a single polarity (up to 4,000 gauss), a sunspot represents a comparatively cool depression (at a temperature of approximately 4,500° C).

Supergiant: A star that is much, much brighter and larger than our Sun. An extremely luminous star of large diameter and low density. A supergiant is the largest known type of star; some are almost as large as our entire solar system. Betelgeuse and Rigel are supergiants.

Supernova: A supernova is a huge explosion that occurs at the end of a mid- to heavyweight star's life. A supernova releases a tremendous amount of energy, expelling the outer layers of the star and becoming extremely bright. What remains is a neutron star or a black hole.

Telescope: A telescope is a device that makes faraway objects appear closer and larger, allowing us to see distant objects in space. The first refracting telescope was invented by Hans Lippershey in 1608.

Trapezium, The: The Trapezium is a star cluster located in the center of the Orion nebula.

UX Tau A: A young star that may only be a million years young.

Veil Nebula: Contains the remains of a supernova that imploded aeons ago. It is 1,500 light-years from Earth.

W. M. Keck Telescope: The famed telescope atop Mauna Kea in Hawaii.

Whirlpool Galaxy (M51): is an interacting grand-design spiral galaxy located at a distance of approximately 23 million light-years in the constellation Canes Venatici.

CREDITS

The following abbreviations are for all images credited to the Hubble and Spitzer telescopes as well as all the associated teams and institutions.

ACS - Advanced Camera for Surveys team
ASU - Arizona State University
AURA – Associated Universities for Research in Astronomy
COBE – Cosmic Background Explorer Satellite
CXC – Chandra X-Ray Center
ESO – European Southern Observatory
ESA - European Space Agency
DFSC – Goddard Spaceflight center
HHT – Hubble Heritage Team
HUDF – Hubble Ultra Deep Field
JPL - Jet Propulsion Laboratory
STScl – the Space Telescope Institute
SSC - Spitzer Science Center
UA - University of Arizona
UBC - University of British Columbia
UM – University of Minn.
UW – University of Wisconsin

Image Credits

Page 40 >NASA: 42 >NASA/JPL-Caltech: 44 >NASA/WMAP Science Team: 46 >NASA, ESA,HHT, (STScI/AURA) - ESA/Hubble Collaboration: 48 >NASA, HHT, (STScI/AURA): 50 > NASA/JPL-Caltech/R. Hurt (SSC): 52 >NASA, ESA, S. Beckwith (STScI) HUDF Team: 54 >NASA, HHT, (STScI/AURA): 56 >J.P. Harrington, K.J. Borkowski (Univ of MD), and NASA 58 >NASA/JPL-Caltech/K. Su (Univ. of Ariz.):

60 >NASA/JPL-Caltech/N. Flagey (IAS/SSC) & A. Noriega-Crespo (SSC/Caltech): 62 > NASA,HHT, (STScI/AURA): 64 > NASA and Adolf Schaller (for STScI): 66 > NASA/CXC/ M.Weiss:
68 > NASA/CXC/M.Weiss: 70 > Robert Gendler 74 > NASA/JPL-Caltech/T. Pyle (SSC): 76 > NASA/JPL-Caltech/T. Pyle (SSC):78 > NASA/JPL-Caltech/T. Pyle (SSC): 80 > NASA/JPL-Caltech/R. Hurt (SSC): 82 > NASA/JPL-Caltech/R. Hurt: 84, 86, 88, 90 > NASA/JPL-Caltech/T. Pyle (SSC): 92, 94 > NASA 96 > Don Davis, NASA: 98 > NASA: 126, 128 > Quills Design: 140 > X-ray: NASA/CXC/J.Hester (ASU); Optical: NASA/ESA/J.Hester & A.Loll (ASU); Infrared: NASA/JPL-Caltech/R.Gehrz (Univ. Minn.): 144 > NASA/JPL-Caltech/E. Churchwell (UW):
146 > NASA, ESA, S. Beckwith, HHT, (STScI/AURA): 148 > NASA, A. Fruchter and the ERO Team (STScI): 150 > NASA, HHT, (STScI/AURA): 152 > NASA/JPL-Caltech/W. Reach (SSC/Caltech): 154 > NASA, ESA, M. Robberto (STS/ESA), Hubble Space Telescope Orion Treasury Project Team: 156 > NASA, ESA, and B. Whitmore (STScI):
158 > NASA, ESA, HHT, (STScl/AURA)-ESA/Hubble Collaboration:
160 > NASA, ESA, HHT, (STScl/AURA):
162 > NASA, ESA and AURA/Caltech:
164 > NASA/JPL-Caltech/T. Megeath (Harvard-Smithsonian CfA): 166 > NASA:
168 > NASA, HHT, (STScI/AURA):

124 > NASA, ESA, Ann Feild, (STScl)
170 > NASA, HHT, (STScI/AURA):
172 >John Bahcall (Institute for Advanced Study, Princeton), Mike Disney (University of Wales), NASA: 132 > NASA, Ann Feild, STScl: 176 > NASA: 178 > NASA, H. Ford (JHU), G. Illingworth (USCS/LO), M. Clampin (STScI), G. Hartig (STScI), ACS Science Team: 180 > NASA: 142 > NASA, ESA, SAO, CXC, JPL-Caltech, STScl: 182 > NASA: 184 > C.R. O'Dell (Rice University), NASA: 186 > NASA, NOAO, ESA, the Hubble Helix Nebula Team, M. Meixner (STScI), and T.A. Rector (NRAO): 188 > NASA, ESA and J. Hester (ASU): 190 > NASA, J. Hester and P. Scowen (ASU): 192 > NASA, HHT (STScI/AURA)-ESA/Hubble Collaboration: 194 > NASA / JPL-Caltech / O. Krause (Steward Observatory): 196 > NASA/JPL-Caltech/L. Allen (Harvard-Smithsonian Center for Astrophysics): 198 > NASA and A. Riess (STScl): 200 > NASA:
202 > NASA/CXC/CfA/R.Kraft et al:
204 > NASA, HHT, (STScI/AURA):
206 > NASA, HHT, (STScI/AURA):
208 > NASA, ESA, S. Beckwith (STScl) and the HUDF Team:

NASA News Releases

41 > http://hubblesite.org/the_telescope/hubble_essentials/
43 > http://planetquest.jpl.nasa.gov/Spitzer/spitzer_index.cfm
45 > http://www.jwst.nasa.gov/firstlight.html
47 > http://hubblesite.org/newscenter/archive/releases/nebula/planetary/1995/01/results/100/
49 > http://hubblesite.org/newscenter/archive/releases/2007/04/image/a/
53 > http://www.spitzer.caltech.edu/news/222-ssc2005-22-Scientists-See-Light-that-May-Be-from-First-Objects-in-Universe
51 > http://hubblesite.org/newscenter/archive/releases/2004/10/image/a/
55 > http://hubblesite.org/newscenter/archive/releases/2004/07/

57 > http://hubblesite.org/newscenter/archive/releases/2003/28/image/a/
59 > http://www.nasa.gov/mission_s/spitzer/news/spitzer-20070212.html
61 > http://www.spitzer.caltech.edu/images/1708-ssc2007-01a-Cosmic-Epic-Unfolds-in-Infrared-The-Eagle-Nebula
63 > http://hubblesite.org/newscenter/archive/releases/1999/41/image/a/
65 > http://www.nasaimages.org/luna/servlet/detail/NVA2~8~8~13363~113904:Hubble-Uncovers-Oldest--Clocks--in-
67 > http://hubblesite.org/newscenter/archive/releases/1999/30/text/
75 > http://www.spitzer.caltech.edu/news/216-ssc2005-15-Spitzer-Finds-Life-Components-in-Young-Universe
77 > http://www.spitzer.caltech.edu/images/1857-ssc2007-16b-Dust-in-the-Quasar-Wind
79 > http://www.spitzer.caltech.edu/images/1845-ssc2007-14c-Steamy-Solar-System
81 > http://www.spitzer.caltech.edu/images/2846-ssc2009-21b-Dusty-Beginnings-of-a-Star
83 > http://www.spitzer.caltech.edu/images/1852-ssc2007-14d-Planet-Forming-Disk-Around-a-Baby-Star
85 > http://www.spitzer.caltech.edu/news/226-ssc2005-26-Partial-Ingredients-for-DNA-and-Protein-Found-Around-Star
87 > http://www.spitzer.caltech.edu/images/1791-ssc2007-08c-Evaporating-Protoplanetary-Disk
89 > http://www.spitzer.caltech.edu/images/2097-sig07-023-Planets-Forming-Around-a-Sun-like-Star
91 > http://www.spitzer.caltech.edu/news/182-ssc2004-22-Spitzer-and-Hubble-Capture-Evolving-Planetary-Systems
141 > http://hubblesite.org/newscenter/archive/releases/2005/37/image/a/
143 > http://hubblesite.org/newscenter/archive/releases/2009/25/image/h/
145 > http://www.spitzer.caltech.edu/images/1170-ssc2004-08a-Stellar-Jewels-Shine-in-New-Spitzer-Image

147 > http://hubblesite.org/newscenter/
archive/releases/2005/12/image/a/

149 > http://hubblesite.org/newscenter/
archive/releases/2000/07/image/a/

151 > http://www.nasa.gov/multimedia/
imagegallery/image_feature_864.html

153 > http://www.spitzer.caltech.edu/
images/1058-ssc2003-06b-Dark-Globule-
in-IC-1396

155 > http://hubblesite.org/newscenter/
archive/releases/2006/01/image/a/

157 > http://www.spitzer.caltech.edu/
images/3244-sig10-017-Takes-Two-
Antenna-Galaxies-to-Tangle

159 > http://hubblesite.org/newscenter/
archive/releases/2007/30/image/a/

161 > http://hubblesite.org/newscenter/
archive/releases/2005/01/image/a/

163 > http://hubblesite.org/newscenter/
archive/releases/2004/20/image/a/

165 > http://www.spitzer.caltech.edu/news
/155-ssc2004-02-Spitzer-Telescope-
Sends-Rose-for-Valentine-s-Day

169 > http://hubblesite.org/newscenter/
archive/releases/2000/10/image/a/

171 > http://hubblesite.org/newscenter/
archive/releases/2004/04/image/a/

175 > http://www.spitzer.caltech.edu/
images/1783-ssc2007-08a-Heart-of-the-
Rosette-Nebula

179 > http://hubblesite.org/newscenter/
archive/releases/2002/11/image/b/

183 > http://www.nasa.gov/vision/uni-
verse/watchtheskies/swift_nsu_0205.html

185 > http://hubblesite.org/newscenter/
archive/releases/1992/29/text/

187 > http://hubblesite.org/newscenter/
archive/releases/2003/11/image/b/

189 > http://hubblesite.org/newscenter/
archive/releases/2003/13/image/a/

191 > http://hubblesite.org/newscenter/
archive/releases/1995/44/image/b/

193 > http://hubblesite.org/newscenter/
archive/releases/2007/41/image/a/

195 > http://www.spitzer.caltech.edu/
news/215-ssc2005-14-NASA-s-Spitzer-
Captures-Echo-of-Dead-Star-s-
Rumblings

197 > http://www.spitzer.caltech.edu/
images/1889-ssc2008-03a-Young-Stars-
in-Their-Baby-Blanket-of-Dust

203 > http://www.nasa.gov/mission_s/
chandra/multimedia/photos08-004.html

205 > http://chandra.harvard.edu/photo/
2009/b1509/

207 > http://hubblesite.org/newscenter/
archive/releases/nebula/emis-
sion/2002/05/image/a/

209 > http://hubblesite.org/newscenter/
archive/releases/2004/07/image/a/

Websites to visit for additional information:

http://HubbleRevealsCreation.com

http://www.youtube.com/watch?v=1KMd-
5MVF_E

http://TheSecretDoorway.com

http://hubblesite.org/

http://www.spitzer.caltech.edu/

http://www.jpl.nasa.gov/

http://kepler.nasa.gov/

http://www.nasa.gov/

http://www.jwst.nasa.gov/

http://www.eso.org/public/

http://www.worldwidetelescope.org/Home.
aspx

http://amazing-space.stsci.edu/resources/
explorations/groundup/

http://chandra.harvard.edu/

http://www.esa.int/esaMI/Planck/SEMWN
20YUFF_0.html

http://oceancolor.gsfc.nasa.gov/SeaWiFS/
HTML/SeaWiFS.BiosphereAnimation.
70W.html

Scriptural Quote: Isaiah 40: 25, 26:
Genesis 1:1-3 New Living Translation

INDEX